70+ SIMPLE RECIPES FC
AND FLAVORFUL WEEKNI(

ONE-POT
MEDITERRANEAN

SAMANTHA FERRARO

AUTHOR OF *THE WEEKNIGHT*
MEDITERRANEAN KITCHEN AND FOUNDER OF
THE LITTLE FERRARO KITCHEN

PAGE STREET
PUBLISHING CO.

First published in 2023 by
Page Street Publishing Co.
27 Congress Street, Suite 1511
Salem, MA 01970
www.pagestreetpublishing.com

Distributed by Macmillan, sales in Canada by The Canadian Manda Group.

27   26   25   24   23   1 2 3 4 5

ISBN-13: 978-1-64567-984-4

ISBN-10: 1-64567-984-5

Library of Congress Control Number: 2022946895

Photography by Samantha Ferraro. Author photos on pages 6 and 165 by Kelsey Kurtis.
Cover and book design by Meg Baskis for Page Street Publishing Co.

Printed and bound in the United States

Page Street Publishing protects our planet by donating to nonprofits like The Trustees, which focuses on local land conservation.

DEDICATION

To Joe, my #1 fan.

CONTENTS

CHAPTER 3
FRESH AND FRAGRANT SEAFOOD RECIPES | 63

CHAPTER 4
COLORFUL AND HEARTY VEGETABLE MAINS | 89

CHAPTER 5
GRAINS, BEANS AND SOME PASTA, TOO | 117

CHAPTER 6
FRESH AND CRISP SALADS ON THE SIDE | 141

INTRODUCTION

ENJOY THE FLAVORS OF THE MEDITERRANEAN, ONE POT AT A TIME

It's been nearly five years since my first cookbook came out and—I can't believe I'm about to say this—ten years since I published the first recipe on my website. I've lived in a handful of different places in my life. I started out a Jewish girl from Brooklyn; then my mom and I moved to the beautiful Big Island of Hawaii, which in the later years is where I met my husband; then we moved to Southern California; and now we call the Pacific Northwest our home. After living in all those beautiful places, I have been lucky enough to experience so much diversity in food and culture and continually work to incorporate those experiences into my everyday cooking.

I am originally from New York, with Sephardic heritage, and I thank my mom for introducing me to unique flavors and opening up my palate to flavors that I now love. I was eating tangy baba ghanoush for as long as I can remember and rolling grape leaves as soon as I had the dexterity. Then when we moved to Hawaii when I was a teenager, I truly experienced what eating from the land meant. I'll never forget the day a local farmer gifted us with a box full of fresh lettuce with green leaves that were almost too pretty to eat. And I thought to myself, *This is what it is all about, doing what you love and sharing it with as many people as you can.* Now, living in the Pacific Northwest, I am surrounded by not only the beautiful scenery, but also loads of locally farmed proteins from pasture-raised animals and bountiful seasonal farmers' markets where you can't help but want to cook everything you see.

Food has always been my love language. Everything from seeing how food is grown and harvested to experiencing other cultures and flavors. I have always said that if there is anything I cook or share that inspires you to try something new, my work here is done! Try new flavors, experiment and adjust to your liking—that is what cooking is all about!

The recipes in this book use approachable ingredients with an emphasis on Mediterranean flavors, inspired from different parts of the Mediterranean, including Spain, Turkey, Italy and Morocco. Having a library of spices on hand instantly transforms a rustic slow-cooked meal into a bright symphony of flavors. Bold spices of smoked paprika, za'atar, cumin and turmeric, just to name a few, give warmth and complexity to the recipes. Once you build your "Mediterranean pantry" of spices and flavorings, the possibilities are endless!

One of the reasons one-pot cooking is so well loved—besides the easier cleanup—is because it's all about building flavors, resulting in a delicious and solid result. One of my absolute favorite dishes to make on the weekends is braised short ribs, quite possibly the epitome of a delicious one-pot meat. Robust cuts of short ribs (page 41) are generously seasoned with an aromatic and earthy spice mixture and seared in a hot Dutch oven until a deep caramelization forms. This is my favorite step in one-pot cooking. The initial sear introduces the depth and flavor for the rest of the dish. Then as the short ribs slowly braise, they become incredibly tender and fall apart, and there is nothing more comforting.

As you are cooking your one-pot recipes, whip up a fresh and crisp salad to complement your meal. I suggest a creamy and crunchy Cucumber Yogurt Salad with Mint and Pistachios (page 143) that would go perfectly alongside Moroccan Meatballs with Saffron Couscous (page 54) or the Lemony Shrimp with Orzo and Asparagus (page 77) served alongside the Citrus Fennel Salad with Orange Blossom Vinaigrette (page 147) for a true explosion of bright flavors.

At the end of the day, my wish for you is to be excited and inspired and to fill your pantry with all of these bold Mediterranean flavors. The premise when cooking Mediterranean, either in one pot or not, is to keep it fresh, vibrant and, most of all, delicious!

A NOTE ON DUTCH OVENS

One of the first cooking investments I ever made was a 6.75-quart (6-L) oval Le Creuset Dutch oven—a stunning piece of cookery that is used time and time again in recipes, and happily displays on my kitchen shelf.

The allure of low-and-slow Dutch oven cooking is that it gives heartier cuts of protein a good amount of time to break down connective tissue and for flavorful sauces to reduce. The tight-fitting lid locks in moisture, keeping proteins juicy and flavorful, and as everything simmers, the meat becomes incredibly tender. This can take time, but the result will be worth the wait.

Dutch ovens can easily be transferred from the stovetop to a hot oven, displayed as the centerpiece on the dinner table and used in a multitude of cooking techniques, such as braising, searing and frying.

Any size or shape of Dutch oven will work for these recipes, but depending on what you are making, the shape can make a slight difference. Wide Dutch ovens called braisers have shorter sides and a wider bottom, which gives ample room for the protein to caramelize. The shallow sides allow moisture to evaporate easily. On the other hand, Dutch ovens with high sides are perfect for hearty stews and soups, such as one-pot Moussaka Stew with Potatoes and Zucchini (page 61) or Root Vegetable Tagine with Harissa and Preserved Lemon (page 91). The high sides hold a good amount of stock and are perfect for making large batches of brothy soups and sauces.

CHAPTER 1

AROMATIC CHICKEN RECIPES

If you are learning to dive into the world of one-pot cooking, a well-made one-pot chicken dish is the perfect place to start.

Chicken is a canvas that welcomes bold spices and layers of flavors. The trick to any well-made one-pot chicken recipe is the timing. Is there skin on the chicken? Take the time to render that glorious fat, giving the whole dish a great savory flavor, which will then be used to toast the couscous in the Garlic-Lemon Chicken with Saffron Pearl Couscous and Zucchini (page 26) to a beautiful golden and nutty hue. Once that layer of flavor is built, herbs and spices continue to add complexity, resulting in a burst of flavors coming from a single pot.

On any given weeknight, you will often find me cooking the Greek Chicken with Rice and Olives (page 13), which utilizes my freezer stash of chicken parts and pantry staples that I always have on hand, including olives and basmati rice.

Another way to add incredible flavor is to marinate the chicken. Yogurt and lemon are both fantastic tenderizers, and, when mixed with earthy turmeric and a good squeeze of fresh lemon, there is not much more that needs to be done except to throw it on a sheet pan for the Lemony Sheet Pan Shish Tawook (page 37). Serve with a fresh and bright chopped salad and warmed pita, and your weeknight dinner is ready.

These chicken recipes are full of fresh, aromatic flavors that come from favorite Mediterranean spices. Saffron, turmeric, cardamom and cumin are all seasonings that transform classic chicken into something bold and lively.

GREEK CHICKEN WITH RICE AND OLIVES

YIELDS
4
servings

This weeknight recipe boasts classic Greek-inspired flavors of fresh herbs, lemon and olives. Both Kalamata and Castelvetrano olives are used in this recipe, but you can use all Kalamata or all Castelvetrano based on what's available to you. The Kalamata olives are much more pungent and brinier compared to the mild and buttery Castelvetrano olives, and the combination of the two varieties gives great flavor that is not too overpowering.

2 lb (907 g) bone-in, skin-on chicken thighs

4 sprigs fresh oregano, finely chopped, divided

4 sprigs fresh rosemary, leaves finely chopped, divided

3 cloves garlic, minced, divided

½ tsp kosher salt

Olive oil, as needed

1 small yellow onion, diced

1 red bell pepper, seeded and chopped into ½-inch (1.3-cm) cubes

1 cup (200 g) uncooked basmati rice

2¼ cups (540 ml) chicken stock

½ cup (90 g) pitted Castelvetrano olives, roughly chopped

½ cup (90 g) pitted Kalamata olives, roughly chopped

1 lemon, thinly sliced

4 oz (113 g) crumbled feta, for garnish

Chopped fresh parsley or cilantro leaves, for garnish

Preheat the oven to 400°F (204°C).

Season the chicken with half of the oregano and rosemary, 1 minced garlic clove and the salt, rubbing the mixture all over the chicken thighs. Set the chicken aside to marinate.

Meanwhile, heat a Dutch oven over medium heat, and drizzle with olive oil. Add the chicken thighs skin side down, and cook until the skin is golden brown, 5 to 7 minutes. Flip the chicken over, and cook for another 3 to 4 minutes. Once both sides of the chicken are deep in color, remove and set aside. In the same skillet, add the onion and bell pepper, and sauté until softened, 3 to 4 minutes.

Add the rest of the oregano, rosemary and garlic, and sauté for another few minutes until the vegetables are aromatic. Stir in the basmati rice, making sure all the rice is coated with the herbs and aromatics and the rice becomes lightly toasted.

Use a spatula to even out the rice, and nestle the chicken thighs back into the rice. Pour the stock in, making sure to not pour directly over the chicken, and scatter the chopped olives and lemon slices on top.

Cover the Dutch oven and roast for 20 minutes. Then remove the lid, and continue cooking for 10 minutes, until the rice is tender and the chicken is cooked through.

Remove the Dutch oven from the oven, and while the chicken is still warm, garnish with crumbled feta and a sprinkle of parsley or cilantro.

 TIP: If your oven has a broiler, place the dish under the broiler for the last few minutes of cooking to crisp the chicken skin.

GOLDEN TURMERIC CHICKEN SOUP WITH DRIED LIME

YIELDS
4
servings

This golden turmeric chicken soup is my mom's sister's recipe, and since making it for the first time over ten years ago, it has become a staple in our house. What makes this soup so special is the addition of Persian dried lime. These are hard, hollow, dried limes that can be found in Mediterranean markets and online. They are aromatic and citrusy, and when added to soups and stews, they permeate the entire dish with lovely floral and acidic notes.

2 tbsp (30 ml) olive oil

½ yellow or white onion, finely chopped

2 cloves garlic, finely chopped

5 cups (1.2 L) low-sodium chicken stock

3 to 4 dried Persian limes

2 tbsp (14 g) turmeric

½ tsp ground black pepper

1 cup (200 g) uncooked basmati rice

1 (15.5-oz [439-g]) can chickpeas, drained and rinsed

1 cup (140 g) cooked shredded chicken

Chopped fresh parsley leaves, for garnish

Heat a Dutch oven over medium heat, and add the olive oil. Add the onion, and sauté for 4 to 5 minutes until soft but not caramelized. Add the garlic, and sauté for another minute.

Pour in the chicken stock, add the dried limes, turmeric, black pepper, basmati rice and chickpeas, and cook until the rice is tender, about 15 minutes. Reduce the heat to low, add the chicken and cook until the chicken is warmed through.

Remove the dried limes and discard before serving. Ladle the soup into bowls, and garnish with parsley.

TIPS: After you make the Dutch Oven Roast Chicken with Preserved Lemon Compound Butter (page 21), save any leftover chicken meat to add to this soup.

If dried limes are difficult to find, you can use lemon peel. Using a vegetable peeler, peel three to four strips of lemon peel, and add them to the soup to steep.

DUTCH OVEN CAPRESE CHICKEN

YIELDS
4
servings

There is not a caprese that I don't enjoy. At the peak of summer when cherry tomatoes are sweet and ripe and basil is fragrant, I look for creative ways to incorporate the season's harvest. This Dutch Oven Caprese Chicken utilizes the garden's bounty into an aromatic and easy one-pot chicken dinner that is full of fresh flavors.

2 boneless, skinless chicken breasts

½ tsp sweet paprika

½ tsp dried oregano

½ tsp dried thyme

1 tsp kosher salt

⅛ tsp ground black pepper

3 tbsp (45 ml) olive oil

2 shallots, cut into thin wedges

3 cloves garlic, minced

1 pint (298 g) cherry tomatoes, larger ones cut in half

½ cup (120 ml) dry white wine, such as Pinot Grigio

4 oz (113 g) mozzarella, sliced

1 cup (24 g) fresh basil, for garnish

Prep the chicken breasts by cutting the breasts in half horizontally. Place each half between a sheet of plastic wrap, and pound the chicken breast to an even thickness.

Season all four chicken cutlets with paprika, oregano, thyme, salt and pepper on both sides.

Heat a wide Dutch oven over medium-high heat, and add the olive oil. Add the chicken cutlets, and sear on the first side for 3 minutes until deeply golden brown. Flip over, and sear the other side for another 2 to 3 minutes, then remove the breasts and set them aside.

Add the shallots, and sauté for 2 to 3 minutes until softened. Stir in the garlic, and sauté for another minute until the garlic is softened and fragrant. Add the cherry tomatoes, and continue sautéing for 3 to 4 minutes until the tomatoes begin to burst and release their juices. Pour in the wine, and use a wooden spoon to scrape any bits that were formed on the bottom. Let the wine reduce for 1 to 2 minutes.

Nestle the chicken cutlets into the tomato mixture, and top the chicken with slices of mozzarella. Place the Dutch oven under the broiler for 3 to 5 minutes, until the cheese is melted and bubbly.

Remove the Dutch oven from the oven, and scatter the fresh basil over the top. Spoon the burst tomatoes and pan sauce over the caprese chicken, and serve.

 TIP: Often grocery stores sell chicken tenders or chicken cutlets where most of the prep is already done. If you find those cuts of chicken, it will save you the prep time of cutting it yourself.

CARDAMOM CHICKEN THIGHS WITH BASMATI RICE AND PINE NUTS

YIELDS
4
servings

Cinnamon is not only for sweet recipes. It is a fantastic addition to savory recipes and used in a multitude of Mediterranean recipes. A little goes a long way, so don't go overboard, but a small pinch of cinnamon with other warm flavors like coriander and cardamom makes a standard chicken and rice dish into something warm and comforting.

Serve with the Turkish Shepherd's Salad with Fresh Herbs and Sumac (page 160) for a truly flavorful meal.

2 tbsp (30 ml) olive oil, plus more as needed

½ cup (68 g) pine nuts

1 tsp cardamom

½ tsp ground cinnamon

½ tsp coriander

¾ tsp kosher salt

½ tsp ground black pepper

2 lb (907 g) bone-in, skin-on chicken thighs

1 medium shallot, finely chopped

2 cloves garlic, minced

1 cup (200 g) uncooked basmati rice

2¼ cups (540 ml) chicken stock

Chopped fresh parsley leaves, for garnish

Sumac, for garnish

Heat a wide Dutch oven over medium heat, and add the olive oil. Add the pine nuts, making sure they are in an even layer, and sauté until all the pine nuts are lightly golden brown. As soon as the color changes, turn off the heat, and transfer the pine nuts to another bowl. Set aside.

In a small bowl, combine the cardamom, cinnamon, coriander, salt and pepper. Pat the chicken dry with paper towels. Sprinkle the spice mixture onto the chicken thighs, making sure all sides are coated evenly.

Heat the Dutch oven over medium heat, and sear the chicken, skin side down, until the skin is a deep golden brown. Turn the chicken over, and continue cooking for another 2 to 3 minutes. Remove the chicken from the Dutch oven, and set aside.

Add the shallot and sauté until translucent, 4 to 5 minutes, adding more oil if needed. Stir in the garlic, and sauté for another minute. Add the basmati rice, and stir it around so all the grains are coated with the oil, then spread the rice into a single layer, and pour in the chicken stock. Nestle the chicken into the Dutch oven, and bring everything to a simmer. Cover the Dutch oven with the lid, and cook for 20 minutes until the chicken is cooked through. For a crispier skin, remove the lid and place the Dutch oven under the broiler for 2 to 3 minutes more.

Once done, fluff the rice with a fork, add the toasted pine nuts and garnish with parsley and sumac.

DUTCH OVEN ROAST CHICKEN WITH PRESERVED LEMON COMPOUND BUTTER

YIELDS
4 to 6
servings

There is something to be said about roasting chicken in a Dutch oven. Dutch ovens retain heat very well, keeping the meat incredibly tender without drying out the leaner cuts, such as the chicken breast. Once the lid is removed, the skin gets perfectly crisp during the final stage of cooking.

Preserved lemon is the star of the compound butter, which is aromatic and flavorful. You can often find preserved lemons in most grocery stores near the pickles or olives. If you can't find preserved lemons, substitute with the zest and juice of one whole lemon.

1 (3- to 4-lb [1.4- to 1.8-kg]) whole chicken, free range if possible

½ yellow onion, quartered

Fresh rosemary, thyme and/or mint sprigs

½ lemon, cut into wedges

1 head garlic, cut in half

¼ cup (60 ml) water

¼ cup (60 ml) dry white wine, such as Pinot Grigio

COMPOUND BUTTER

4 tbsp (60 g) unsalted butter, softened

½ preserved lemon, seeds removed, finely chopped

3 cloves garlic, grated or finely chopped

2 sprigs fresh rosemary, leaves finely chopped

3 to 4 sprigs fresh thyme, leaves finely chopped

2 sprigs fresh mint, leaves finely chopped

2 tbsp (30 ml) olive oil

½ tsp turmeric

½ tsp paprika

1 tsp kosher salt

½ tsp ground black pepper

Preheat the oven to 425°F (218 °C), and place the oven rack in the lower center of the oven. Pat the chicken dry very well with paper towels to help the butter and seasonings stick to the meat better. Remove any gizzards from the chicken cavity, and set aside.

To make the compound butter, in a medium bowl, add the butter, preserved lemon, garlic, rosemary, thyme, mint, olive oil, turmeric, paprika, salt and pepper, and mix to combine. Alternatively, you can also add the compound butter ingredients to a small food processor, and pulse to combine.

Slather the compound butter all over the chicken and carefully under the skin so the entire chicken is evenly coated. Fill the cavity with the onion, fresh herbs and lemon, and tie the legs together with butcher's twine. (You can also do this with a strip of aluminum foil.) Place the chicken breast side up in the Dutch oven. Nestle the head of garlic alongside the chicken, and pour the water and white wine around the chicken.

Place the Dutch oven in the oven, and roast the chicken, uncovered, for 40 to 45 minutes. Place the lid on the Dutch oven, and continue roasting until the internal temperature of the chicken reaches 165°F (74°C), about another 30 minutes.

Once the chicken is done, remove it from the oven, and let it cool for at least 10 minutes so the juices can redistribute. Carve the chicken, and spread the softened roasted cloves garlic onto the chicken, for serving.

TIP: Some recipes suggest using just the preserved lemon's peel in recipes because it will be less salty than the flesh. However, not all brands preserve the same way. Taste a piece of the lemon and, if you like, add both the peel and flesh to the recipe, which is what I like to do.

HERBY CHICKEN WITH FARRO AND SUN-DRIED TOMATOES

I love incorporating farro into one-pot recipes because it offers a nutty, filling and chewy component. Farro is a great source of fiber and antioxidants, and it takes on any flavor that you give it, such as dried herbs and savory sun-dried tomatoes.

3 tbsp (45 ml) olive oil, plus more as needed

2 lb (907 g) boneless, skinless chicken thighs, cut into 1-inch (2.5-cm) pieces

½ tsp dried oregano

½ tsp dried thyme

1 tsp kosher salt

½ tsp ground black pepper

1 large leek, white and light green parts only, thinly sliced

2 cloves garlic, minced

½ cup (120 ml) dry white wine, such as Pinot Grigio

1 cup (150 g) farro

2½ cups (600 ml) chicken stock

½ cup (27 g) sun-dried tomatoes, roughly chopped

Lemon wedges, for garnish

Fresh thyme leaves, for garnish

Fresh parsley leaves, for garnish

Grated Parmesan cheese, for garnish

Preheat the oven to 425°F (218°C), and heat a Dutch oven over high heat. Add the olive oil.

Season the chicken thighs with the oregano, thyme, salt and pepper on all sides. When the oil is hot, add the chicken to the Dutch oven, and sear until the chicken is deeply caramelized on both sides. Remove the chicken, and set aside.

In the same Dutch oven, add more oil if needed, and sauté the leeks until softened, 8 to 10 minutes. Stir in the garlic, and sauté for another minute. Pour in the white wine, and use a spatula to scrape off any meaty bits from the bottom of the pot. Let the wine reduce for another 30 seconds.

Stir in the farro, and sauté until all of the farro is coated with the infused oil and aromatics.

Pour in the chicken stock, and add the chicken back in with any accumulated juices. Spread the farro and chicken out in an even layer, and scatter the sun-dried tomatoes all over.

Cover, and bring everything up to a boil. Once boiling, remove from the heat, and place the Dutch oven in the oven. Cook for 35 to 40 minutes, until the farro is cooked through and the liquid has evaporated. Remove the chicken from the oven, and let it cool for at least 10 minutes.

To serve, garnish with lemon wedges and top with fresh thyme and parsley leaves and a grating of Parmesan cheese.

TIP: When shopping for sun-dried tomatoes, look for ones that are packed in oil. These are more tender and flavorful, and the oil can be used in place of olive oil or added to dressings.

CHICKEN CACCIATORE WITH PEPPERS AND OLIVES

YIELDS
4
servings

Chicken cacciatore is a rustic chicken stew, also known as hunter's stew, with braised chicken simmered in a tomato-based sauce with various vegetables. This is the perfect stew to make depending on which vegetables are in season or what needs to be used. Some variations add carrots, celery or mushrooms. The version I grew up with has hefty slices of sweet bell peppers that are simmered with garlic and onions. A splash of white wine and simmered anchovy fillets add another layer of depth, giving the entire stew great flavor.

While the chicken is simmering, make the Creamy Mascarpone Polenta (page 120) to serve alongside. The rich tomato sauce is a perfect accompaniment to the creamy polenta.

2 to 3 chicken quarters (or 4 bone-in, skin-on chicken thighs)

1 tsp kosher salt

½ tsp ground black pepper

2 tbsp (30 ml) olive oil

1 shallot, thinly sliced

2 red or orange bell peppers, core removed, sliced

3 cloves garlic, finely chopped

1 tsp dried oregano

1 tsp dried thyme

½ tsp red pepper flakes

3 anchovy fillets

2 tbsp (32 g) tomato paste

½ cup (120 ml) dry white wine, such as Pinot Grigio

1 (32-oz [907-g]) can crushed tomatoes

1 cup (180 g) pitted Castelvetrano olives

Chopped fresh parsley leaves, for garnish

Pat the chicken dry very well with paper towels, and season with salt and pepper on all sides. Heat a wide Dutch oven over medium-high heat, and add the olive oil. Sear the chicken on both sides until golden brown. Remove and set aside.

Add the shallot and bell peppers to the Dutch oven, and sauté until just softened, 2 to 3 minutes. Stir in the garlic, oregano, thyme and red pepper flakes, and sauté for another minute, making sure the spices are thoroughly mixed in. Add the anchovy fillets and tomato paste, and stir into the oil, using a spatula to break down the anchovy so it melts into the fat.

Pour in the white wine, scraping off any residual bits from the bottom of the Dutch oven. Let the wine reduce for another minute, and give everything a good mix. Pour in the tomatoes, and stir everything together so the vegetables are evenly dispersed. Return the chicken and any accumulated juices into the tomato sauce mixture.

Place the lid on, leaving a small opening, and bring everything to a boil. Once boiling, reduce the heat to a simmer, and cook for 50 to 55 minutes, until the chicken is incredibly tender and the sauce has reduced. Remove the lid, scatter the olives around the chicken and cook uncovered for another 5 minutes.

Garnish the chicken cacciatore with the parsley, and serve the braised chicken with the sauce, peppers and olives.

GARLIC-LEMON CHICKEN WITH SAFFRON PEARL COUSCOUS AND ZUCCHINI

YIELDS
4
servings

If you are looking to break into the world of fennel, this is a great recipe to start. Fennel is one of my favorite vegetables, and when cooked with chicken and other aromatics such as thyme and lemon, the fennel transforms from sharp to caramelized and sweet.

CHICKEN MARINADE

2 lb (907 g) bone-in, skin-on chicken thighs

4 garlic gloves, finely chopped or grated

1 tsp dried thyme

½ tsp cumin

1 tsp kosher salt

½ tsp ground black pepper

½ lemon, zested and juiced

¼ cup plus 2 tbsp (90 ml) olive oil, divided

PEARL COUSCOUS

Pinch of saffron

1 tbsp (15 ml) warm water

1 shallot, diced

1 medium fennel bulb, diced

2 tbsp (32 g) tomato paste

½ cup (120 ml) dry white wine, such as Pinot Grigio

2 medium zucchini, diced

1 cup (150 g) dried pearl couscous

2½ cups (600 ml) low-sodium chicken stock

Chopped fresh parsley leaves, for garnish

Pat the chicken thighs dry with paper towels, and season with the chopped garlic, thyme, cumin, salt, pepper, lemon zest, lemon juice and ¼ cup (60 ml) of olive oil. Use your hands to evenly coat the chicken all over, and set aside. If you have the time, marinate for at least 20 minutes and up to 8 hours.

While the chicken marinates, preheat the oven to 375°F (190°C), and add a pinch of saffron to the warm water to steep while you prepare the rest of the recipe.

Heat a wide Dutch oven over medium to high heat, and drizzle with the remaining 2 tablespoons (30 ml) of olive oil. Place the chicken thighs in the Dutch oven, skin side down, and sear the chicken until the skin is a deep golden color, then flip over and cook the other side for 3 to 4 minutes. Once the chicken is seared on both sides, transfer it to a plate.

To make the couscous, to the same Dutch oven, add the shallot and fennel, and sauté for 2 to 3 minutes to soften. Stir in the tomato paste and saffron water, and use a spatula to break up the paste so it melts into the oil. Next, pour in the white wine, and use a spatula to scrape any meaty bits from the bottom. Add the zucchini and couscous, and pour in the chicken stock. Give everything a gentle mix to evenly distribute all of the ingredients.

Return the chicken, skin side up, and any accumulated juices into the Dutch oven.

Cover and position the Dutch oven on the middle rack in the oven, and cook for 25 to 28 minutes, until at least half of the liquid has absorbed. Remove the lid, and continue cooking for 8 to 10 minutes, until the chicken is cooked through and golden brown and the pearl couscous is tender.

Garnish the chicken with parsley, and serve the chicken with the couscous and vegetables.

LEMONY ZA'ATAR CHICKEN AND POTATOES

YIELDS
4
servings

Za'atar is a flavorful spice blend with bold additions of citrusy sumac and sesame seeds. Today, the blend is easily found in standard grocery stores, and I highly recommend adding za'atar to your spice collection.

Za'atar is not only a fantastic rub on chicken, but it goes very well in Green Shakshuka with Za'atar and Feta (page 104). You can also mix za'atar with some olive oil and brush it onto warm pita, which would be a great accompaniment to the Smoky Moroccan Eggplant and Tomato Dip (page 107).

The harissa tahini is optional but highly recommended. Yes, it uses another kitchen tool, but the savory and spicy tahini sauce is the perfect addition to the bold flavors of the roast chicken.

CHICKEN MARINADE

2 lb (907 g) bone-in, skin-on chicken thighs

3 tbsp (45 ml) olive oil

2 tbsp (20 g) za'atar

1 tsp kosher salt

2 cloves garlic, finely chopped or grated

Zest of 1 lemon

Chopped fresh parsley leaves, for garnish

POTATOES

1 lb (454 g) thin-skinned baby potatoes

2 tbsp (30 ml) olive oil

½ tsp sumac

½ tsp kosher salt

½ cup (120 ml) chicken stock

1 lemon, sliced

HARISSA TAHINI SAUCE

½ cup (127 g) tahini paste

½ cup (120 ml) water

1 tsp spicy harissa paste

1 tsp lemon juice

½ tsp kosher salt

¼ tsp cumin

Preheat the oven to 425°F (218°C), and pat the chicken thighs well with a paper towel. Season the chicken with the olive oil, za'atar, salt, garlic and lemon zest, making sure to rub the mixture all over the chicken. Place the chicken thighs into a wide Dutch oven or braising pan, skin side up.

Cut any large baby potatoes in half, and leave the very small ones whole. Season the potatoes with the olive oil, sumac and salt, and scatter the seasoned potatoes all around the chicken. Pour the chicken stock around the chicken and potatoes, and place the lemon slices on top.

Place the Dutch oven onto the middle rack in the oven, and cook, uncovered, for 28 to 30 minutes, until the chicken is cooked through and the potatoes are tender.

While the chicken is cooking, make the harissa tahini sauce. In a small bowl, add the tahini, water, harissa paste, lemon juice, salt and cumin, and whisk until combined and smooth. You can also add all of the ingredients to a small food processor, and blend until smooth and creamy.

Once the chicken is done, remove from the oven and let it rest for at least 5 minutes, then garnish with the parsley and a drizzle of the harissa tahini sauce.

 TIP: This is one of those hands-off roast chicken recipes that I just adore. To make it even easier, season the chicken right in the braising pan, eliminating the need for additional bowls.

BROTHY TUSCAN CHICKEN WITH SUN-DRIED TOMATOES, SPINACH AND ARTICHOKES

YIELDS
4
servings

This recipe is inspired by Tuscan flavors and utilizes everyday pantry staples, including white beans, canned artichoke hearts (though frozen artichoke hearts would work, too) and sun-dried tomatoes. As the beans simmer in the herby tomato broth, they become plump and creamy, providing a delicious layer of texture and flavor to the dish.

2 lb (907 g) bone-in, skin-on chicken thighs

½ tsp kosher salt

½ tsp ground black pepper

1 tsp dried oregano

2 tbsp (30 ml) olive oil

3 cloves garlic, finely chopped

Juice of 1 lemon

¾ cup (180 ml) low-sodium chicken stock

3 cups (90 g) baby spinach

1 (15.5-oz [439-g]) can white beans, drained

1 (14-oz [396-g]) can artichoke hearts, drained and cut in half or quartered

½ cup (27 g) sun-dried tomatoes, with oil

Fresh oregano leaves, for garnish

Preheat the oven to 425°F (218°C).

Pat the chicken thighs dry, and season with salt, black pepper and oregano, making sure the seasonings coat all sides of the chicken.

Heat a wide Dutch oven over medium-high heat, and add the olive oil. Place the chicken, skin side down, and sear until the skin is golden. Turn the chicken over, and continue to cook the other side for another 2 to 3 minutes, until caramelized. Remove the chicken and set aside.

Add the garlic to the pan, and sauté for 1 minute, until just caramelized. Pour in the lemon juice and chicken stock, using a sturdy spatula to scrape any meaty bits from the bottom.

Add the spinach, white beans, artichoke hearts and sun-dried tomatoes, stirring so the mixture is evenly distributed. Return the chicken, skin side up, and any accumulated juices to the pan, nestling among the beans and vegetables. Place the Dutch oven onto the middle rack of the oven.

Roast the chicken, uncovered, for 25 to 28 minutes, until the chicken is cooked through.

Let the chicken rest for at least 5 minutes, and garnish with fresh oregano.

WARM CORIANDER CHICKEN QUARTERS WITH BRAISED LENTILS

YIELDS
4
servings

Braised lentils with aromatic coriander are the star of the show in this recipe. Lentils are hearty, and my tip for cooking brown lentils is to add a splash of citrus or vinegar right at the end. The fresh addition right at the finish instantly wakes up the robust flavors.

Chicken quarters are used in this recipe for creating an incredibly succulent cut that can handle the long braise of lentils.

SPICED CHICKEN

2 bone-in, skin-on chicken leg quarters

1 tsp smoked paprika

½ tsp dried oregano

1 tsp kosher salt

½ tsp ground black pepper

3 tbsp (45 ml) olive oil

BRAISED LENTILS

1 large leek, white and light green parts only, thinly sliced

2 stalks celery, cut into small chunks

2 medium carrots, peeled and cut into small chunks

3 cloves garlic, finely chopped

2 tbsp (32 g) tomato paste

½ tsp cumin

½ tsp coriander

½ tsp smoked paprika

1 cup (192 g) brown lentils

4 cups (960 ml) low-sodium chicken stock

1 tsp kosher salt

½ tsp ground black pepper

2 fresh rosemary sprigs

1 bay leaf

1 tbsp (15 ml) red wine vinegar or lemon juice

Chopped fresh parsley leaves, for garnish

Pat the chicken quarters dry, and season the chicken with the smoked paprika, oregano, salt and pepper, making sure the spices are evenly coated all over the chicken.

Heat a large Dutch oven over medium-high heat, and add the olive oil. Add the chicken skin side down, and sear until a deep golden crust forms, 5 to 6 minutes. These are larger cuts of chicken, so use a spatula or tongs to help press the chicken into the hot oil from time to time. Once the first side is seared, turn the chicken over, and sear the other side. Remove and set aside.

To the Dutch oven, add the leek, and sauté for 4 to 5 minutes to soften. Add the celery and carrots, and continue sautéing for another 2 to 3 minutes.

Stir in the garlic, and continue cooking for another minute until the garlic becomes fragrant.

Add the tomato paste, cumin, coriander and smoked paprika, and stir into the oil, breaking up the tomato paste with a spatula. Add the lentils, giving everything a good stir so the lentils begin to take on all the flavors. Pour in the chicken stock, and season with salt and pepper. Give everything one final stir, and use a spatula to spread everything out into an even layer.

Nestle the chicken into the Dutch oven, making sure the broth comes up halfway but does not completely submerge the chicken. Add the rosemary sprigs and the bay leaf, and bring everything to a boil.

Once boiling, place the lid on, leaving a small opening, and reduce the heat to a constant simmer. Continue simmering for 55 to 60 minutes, until the lentils are tender and the chicken is cooked through and incredibly tender.

As soon as the chicken and lentils are done, stir the red wine vinegar or fresh lemon juice right into the lentils, and garnish with parsley.

LEMONY CHICKEN PICCATA WITH ORZO AND SPINACH

This recipe is a play on chicken piccata. Typically, chicken piccata is made with a lemony caper sauce and served with pasta on the side. Instead, we're taking strong inspiration from that and making the same dish in one pan, thanks to quick-cooking orzo. Because everything happens relatively quickly, thin chicken cutlets are used in this recipe, making for an easy stovetop dinner.

2 tbsp (30 ml) olive oil, plus more as needed

2 tbsp (30 ml) ghee or unsalted butter

½ cup (63 g) all-purpose flour

1 tsp kosher salt

½ tsp ground black pepper

½ tsp dried thyme

2 to 4 boneless, skinless chicken cutlets

3 cloves garlic, finely chopped

8 oz (226 g) dried orzo

½ cup (120 ml) dry white wine, such as Pinot Grigio

¼ cup (60 ml) lemon juice

2½ cups (600 ml) chicken stock

2 cups (60 g) baby spinach

¼ cup (30 g) capers, plus more for garnish

¼ cup (25 g) grated Parmesan cheese, plus more for garnish

Chopped fresh parsley leaves, for garnish

Lemon wedges, for serving

Heat a wide Dutch oven over medium heat, and add the olive oil and ghee, cooking until melted. Season the flour with salt, pepper and thyme, and dredge the chicken cutlets with the seasoned flour. Add the chicken to the Dutch oven, and sear until the chicken is golden brown on both sides and cooked through, 2 to 3 minutes per side. Transfer the chicken to a plate, and cover with aluminum foil to keep warm.

Add more olive oil to the Dutch oven, if needed, and add the garlic, and sauté for 1 minute, until fragrant. Stir the orzo into the flavored oil, making sure all the grains are lightly coated with the oil, and begin to lightly toast for another minute. Pour in the wine, using a spatula to scrape up any meaty bits from the bottom. Add the lemon juice and chicken stock, and give everything a good stir. Continue cooking until the orzo is just cooked through and tender, 10 to 12 minutes.

Turn the heat off, and stir in the spinach, allowing the residual heat to gently wilt the spinach. Add the capers, Parmesan and parsley into the orzo, and stir together until the orzo is creamy and the spinach has wilted.

Right before serving, slice the chicken cutlets, and serve on top of the creamy orzo. Garnish with additional capers, more Parmesan and lemon wedges.

TIP: If you can't find chicken cutlets, you can make them yourself. Cut boneless, skinless chicken breasts in half or in thirds horizontally, and use a mallet to pound the chicken into a very thin and even cutlet. Another option would be to use four to six chicken tenders, which are an incredibly tender cut of chicken and would work very well in this recipe.

LEMONY SHEET PAN SHISH TAWOOK

YIELDS
4
servings

Shish tawook literally translates to "chicken skewers" and is very popular in Lebanese cuisine. Similar to kebabs, this marinade is inspired by bright Lebanese flavors of lemon, tangy yogurt and paprika. Instead of skewering the marinated chicken, we're making this a bit easier for a weeknight dinner and placing the same yogurt-marinated chicken pieces onto a sheet pan and right into a hot oven.

Chickpeas and cherry tomatoes are scattered around the chicken, and as everything roasts, the cherry tomatoes gently burst and the chickpeas become nutty and delicious, making for a complete and flavorful dinner. Serve the chicken tawook with Mediterranean Chopped Salad with Creamy Tahini (page 144) or Cucumber Yogurt Salad with Mint and Pistachios (page 143) and warm pita bread.

CHICKEN MARINADE

2 lb (907 g) boneless, skinless chicken thighs, cut into 1-inch (2.5-cm) pieces

¼ cup (60 ml) plain Greek yogurt

Zest and juice of 1 lemon

2 tbsp (30 ml) olive oil

2 cloves garlic, finely chopped or grated

½ tsp paprika

½ tsp cumin

½ tsp turmeric

1 tsp kosher salt

½ tsp Aleppo pepper

CHICKPEA AND TOMATO MIXTURE

1 (15.5-oz [439-g]) can chickpeas, drained and rinsed

1 pint (298 g) cherry tomatoes, larger ones cut in half

1 small red onion, cut into wedges

3 tbsp (45 ml) olive oil

½ tsp kosher salt

¼ tsp ground black pepper

Chopped fresh parsley or cilantro leaves, for garnish

Preheat the oven to 425°F (218°C), and line a baking sheet with parchment paper or aluminum foil. Add the chicken pieces to a large bowl along with the yogurt, lemon zest and juice, olive oil, garlic, paprika, cumin, turmeric, salt and Aleppo pepper, and give everything a good mix, making sure the yogurt marinade is coated all over the chicken pieces.

Place the chicken on the baking sheet, spreading it out into an even layer. In a medium bowl, combine the chickpeas, cherry tomatoes, red onion, olive oil, salt and pepper, and scatter around the chicken.

Place the sheet pan into the oven, and roast for 20 minutes, until the chicken is just cooked through, the tomatoes are soft and the chickpeas are tender. Place the sheet pan under the broiler for 2 to 3 minutes to crisp the chicken a little bit more. Remove from the oven, and allow the chicken to rest and cool for a few minutes before serving. Garnish with chopped parsley or cilantro.

 TIP: If you have the time, marinate the chicken for at least 20 minutes and up to overnight, which will only add more flavor to the chicken.

CHAPTER 2

COMFORTING BEEF AND LAMB DISHES

I've always said, if I could have one meal for the rest of my life, it would be braised short ribs. There is nothing more comforting than a perfectly braised beef dish with succulent, fall-off-the-bone meat. Short ribs have a lot of connective tissue and need time to cook low and slow to get tender. As you sear the meat, look for the deep caramelization on the fond, which is the meaty bits that get stuck on the bottom of the Dutch oven. This is all flavor, and when you add a liquid to deglaze the pan, you're pulling up that concentrated flavor from the initial sear and bringing it right back into the rest of the dish.

Beef and lamb are heartier cuts of proteins, and these are the cuts that I crave during the cooler months of the year. Because these proteins are robust in flavor, beef and lamb welcome aromatics and spices to complement their rich notes.

Braised Lamb Shanks with Pomegranate and Dried Figs (page 46) is the recipe to make when you want to impress. A cinnamon stick and dried figs are added to the simmering broth, turning the gamier protein into a sweet and savory masterpiece.

And for a recipe that feeds a crowd and is impressive enough to serve around the holidays, try the Braciole Stuffed with Pine Nuts and Parmesan (page 58), which is Italian comfort food. Pounded flank steak is rolled with fresh herbs and pine nuts and braised low and slow in a simple marinara.

TURMERIC-BRAISED SHORT RIBS WITH RED WINE AND DATES

YIELDS
4
servings

There is no other beef cut I love more than well-made braised short ribs. The seasonings in this recipe take inspiration from a blend called *hawaij*, which translates to "mixture" in Arabic. The Middle Eastern blend usually has a concoction consisting of turmeric, cumin and coriander, creating an incredibly fragrant and earthy layer of flavor.

The other main component is date molasses, called *silan* in Hebrew. This is another ingredient that is becoming more well-known in Western stores, and I highly recommend adding it to your collection. Silan is a thick, slightly sweet syrup made from dates and offers a honeyed layer of flavor. If you don't have silan, add a squeeze of honey into liquid, which will also give a slightly sweet and savory combination of flavors.

2 tbsp (30 ml) olive oil

2 tsp (5 g) turmeric

2 tsp (4 g) cumin

1 tsp coriander

2 tsp (10 g) kosher salt, divided

¾ tsp ground black pepper

2½ to 3 lb (1.1 to 1.4 kg) thick-cut short ribs

½ cup (63 g) all-purpose flour

1 red onion, thinly sliced

3 cloves garlic, minced

3 carrots, cut into 1-inch (2.5-cm) pieces

2 cups (480 ml) low-sodium beef stock

1 cup (240 ml) red wine, such as Cabernet Sauvignon

2 tbsp (30 ml) date molasses

1 cup (175 g) pitted Medjool dates, cut in half

Chopped fresh parsley leaves, for garnish

Preheat the oven to 350°F (176°C). Heat a wide Dutch oven over medium-high heat, and add the olive oil.

In a small bowl, combine the turmeric, cumin, coriander, 1 teaspoon of salt and the pepper. Season the short ribs with the spice mixture on all sides, and lightly dredge the short ribs with the flour, making sure all sides are lightly coated.

In batches, sear the short ribs in the hot oil until all sides have a deep caramelized crust, 2 to 3 minutes per side. Remove and set aside. Next, add the onion, and sauté for about 2 minutes, until slightly softened. Add the garlic and carrots, and continue sautéing for another 1 to 2 minutes, until the garlic has softened but not caramelized.

Return the short ribs and any accumulated juices to the Dutch oven. Pour in the beef stock and red wine, and stir in the date molasses. Season everything with the remaining teaspoon of salt, and bring to a simmer. Once simmering, cover the pot, and roast the short ribs in the oven for 2 to 2½ hours. Add the dried dates during the last half hour of cooking.

Once done, the sauce should have reduced slightly, and the short ribs will be fall-off-the-bone tender. Garnish the braised short ribs with chopped parsley, and serve alongside vegetables and the reduced sauce.

 TIP: If working with boneless short ribs, you may need to decrease the cooking time, so keep that in mind. But as soon as the short ribs become fork-tender, they are good to go!

PERSIAN LENTIL MEATBALLS IN SAFFRON BROTH (KOUFTEH)

YIELDS
4 to 6
servings

Also called *koofteh berengi*, these hearty meatballs are filled with split peas, rice and loads of fresh herbs. If you have access to a Middle Eastern store, look for *sabzi koufteh*, which is a blend of dried herbs. Using it saves prep time from chopping the fresh herbs, though I do love the brightness that fresh herbs offer.

KOUFTEH (MEATBALLS)

2 cups (480 ml) water

½ cup (112 g) yellow split peas, soaked (see Tip)

1 lb (454 g) ground beef

½ cup (100 g) uncooked basmati rice, rinsed well

½ onion, grated

½ cup (50 g) finely chopped fresh mint leaves

½ cup (30 g) finely chopped fresh parsley leaves

¼ cup (12 g) finely chopped fresh chives

1 egg

2 tsp (5 g) turmeric

1 tsp dried tarragon

1 tsp coriander

1 tsp kosher salt

½ tsp ground black pepper

TOMATO-SAFFRON BROTH

2 tbsp (30 ml) olive oil

½ onion, thinly sliced

1 clove garlic, finely chopped

2 tbsp (32 g) tomato paste

Pinch of saffron

5 cups (1.2 L) low-sodium vegetable stock

Chopped fresh parsley leaves, for garnish

Lemon wedges, for serving

In a Dutch oven, bring the water to a boil, and add the soaked split peas. Cook for 10 to 12 minutes, until the split peas are halfway cooked through. Then drain and rinse the split peas to cool them down.

In a large bowl, add the ground beef, along with the precooked split peas, basmati rice, grated onion, mint, parsley, chives, egg, turmeric, dried tarragon, coriander, salt and pepper. Give everything a very good mix so everything is well combined with the ground beef. Using your hands, form the mixture into 8 to 10 medium-sized meatballs and set aside.

Heat the same Dutch oven to medium heat, and add the olive oil. Add the sliced onion, and sauté for 3 to 5 minutes, until softened. Add the garlic, and sauté for another minute. Stir in the tomato paste, and sauté for another 30 seconds, using a spatula to really break down the tomato paste into the oil.

Add a pinch of saffron, and pour in the vegetable stock, giving everything a good stir. Add the meatballs one at a time until they are all submerged into the broth. Cover with the lid, and bring to a strong simmer. Cook the meatballs for 40 to 45 minutes, until the rice and split peas are tender.

To serve, ladle the koufteh into wide, shallow bowls, and pour the tomato-saffron broth around the meatballs. Garnish the koufteh with parsley and lemon wedges.

TIP: Split peas take a while to cook, but soaking them ahead helps them cook faster. Right before you start the prep, soak the split peas in warm water for at least 30 minutes, giving them a head start.

TURKISH-SPICED STUFFED PEPPERS

YIELDS
4 to 6
servings

The scent of slowly simmering stuffed peppers is a favorite childhood memory of mine. My mom would often make the same filling for stuffed grape leaves, stuffed peppers and stuffed tomatoes. Though my mom kept her filling very simple, over the years I've adapted it with some of my favorite Turkish flavors. Both the smoked paprika and cumin give the mixture a depth of flavor, and the dried mint brightens everything ever so slightly. This recipe uses ground turkey, which is a little lighter than beef, but you can use ground beef and lamb as well.

STUFFED PEPPERS

1 lb (454 g) ground turkey

¼ cup (50 g) uncooked basmati rice

½ small yellow onion, grated

2 cloves garlic, minced

1½ tsp (4 g) smoked paprika

1 tsp cumin

1 tsp kosher salt

½ tsp dried mint

¼ tsp Aleppo pepper, plus more for garnish

3 large bell peppers of various colors, cut in half and seeds removed

Chopped fresh parsley leaves, for garnish

TOMATO SAUCE

2 cups (480 ml) vegetable stock

2 cups (480 ml) tomato sauce or strained tomatoes

1 tbsp (16 g) tomato paste

¾ tsp kosher salt

½ tsp cumin

½ tsp garlic powder

In a large bowl, combine the ground turkey, basmati rice, onion, garlic, smoked paprika, cumin, salt, mint and Aleppo pepper. Give everything a good mix. Divide the meat mixture evenly among the hollowed-out bell peppers, and place the bell peppers, stuffing side up, in a Dutch oven.

In another large bowl, whisk the vegetable stock, tomato sauce, tomato paste, salt, cumin and garlic powder together. Pour the tomato sauce mixture around the stuffed peppers until just covered. Place the lid on, leaving a small opening, and bring up to a boil, then reduce to a simmer. Continue simmering for 1 hour to 1 hour and 10 minutes, until the peppers are tender and the rice and meat mixture is cooked through.

To serve, spoon the reduced tomato sauce over the stuffed peppers, and garnish with parsley.

BRAISED LAMB SHANKS WITH POMEGRANATE AND DRIED FIGS

YIELDS
4
servings

Braised lamb shanks are such a showstopper of a recipe. Lamb shanks are gamier when it comes to proteins, and they welcome vibrant flavors of fresh herbs, deep spices and tangy pomegranate molasses. The dried figs also simmer in the braising liquid, becoming plump and irresistibly sweet.

2 to 4 lamb shanks, 2 to 3 lb (907 g to 1.4 kg) total

½ tsp cumin

½ tsp coriander

1 tsp kosher salt

½ tsp ground black pepper

2 tbsp (30 ml) olive oil

1 small onion, thinly sliced

2 large carrots, cut into 1-inch (2.5-cm) pieces

1 celery stalk, cut into ½-inch (1.3-cm) pieces

2 cloves garlic, smashed

1 tbsp (16 g) tomato paste

½ cup (120 ml) red wine, such as Cabernet Sauvignon

1½ cups (360 ml) beef or chicken stock

1 tbsp (15 ml) pomegranate molasses

1 cinnamon stick

2 bay leaves

5 to 6 sprigs fresh thyme, tied in a bundle

1 cup (150 g) dried figs

Chopped fresh parsley or cilantro leaves, for garnish

Pomegranate seeds, for garnish

Preheat the oven to 350°F (176°C).

Dry the lamb shanks very well with paper towels. This will help the seasonings stick to the meat.

Season the lamb shanks with the cumin, coriander, salt and pepper, and rub the spices all over the shanks. Heat a wide Dutch oven over high heat, and add the olive oil. Once the oil is hot, sear the lamb shanks on all sides until a deep crust forms, 3 to 4 minutes per side. Once the shanks are deep in color, transfer them to a plate and set aside.

In the same Dutch oven, add the onion, carrots, celery and garlic, and sauté the vegetables for 3 to 5 minutes, until the vegetables begin to soften. Stir in the tomato paste, and sauté for another minute. Pour in the red wine, stock and pomegranate molasses.

Return the shanks and any accumulated juices to the Dutch oven. Nestle the cinnamon stick, bay leaves and thyme bundle into the liquid mixture, and scatter the dried figs around the lamb shanks. Bring everything to a boil. Cover and roast the lamb shanks in the oven until the lamb is tender and the sauce has reduced, 1½ to 2 hours. Depending how thick your lamb shanks are, time may vary, but the meat should easily fall off the bone when cooked through.

Once done, remove from the oven, and let the lamb cool for at least 15 minutes before serving. Discard the cinnamon stick, bay leaves and thyme bundle, and garnish with parsley or cilantro and pomegranate seeds.

 TIP: Lamb shanks can vary in size, and the larger they are, the more time they need to cook low and slow. You'll know it's ready when the meat is incredibly tender and falls off the bone easily.

HERBY KOFTA WITH QUICK TZATZIKI

These mini kofta are such a fun appetizer! I prefer to sear these on the stove, but you can also form the kofta and roast them on a lined baking sheet in the oven. Place the small kofta onto crisp leaves of radicchio and top with this quick and creamy tzatziki. Your guests will be fighting over these.

HERBY KOFTA

½ lb (226 g) ground beef

½ lb (226 g) ground lamb

3 tbsp (30 g) grated onion

2 cloves garlic, finely chopped or grated

2 tbsp (32 g) tomato paste

2 tbsp (8 g) finely chopped fresh parsley leaves

2 tbsp (12 g) finely chopped fresh mint leaves

½ tsp sumac

1 tsp turmeric

½ tsp cumin

½ tsp kosher salt

¼ tsp Aleppo pepper

2 tbsp (30 ml) olive oil

QUICK TZATZIKI

½ cup (120 ml) plain, full-fat Greek yogurt

½ Persian cucumber, grated

2 tbsp (8 g) finely chopped fresh parsley leaves

2 tbsp (12 g) finely chopped fresh mint leaves

1 tbsp (15 ml) lemon juice

¼ tsp kosher salt

FOR SERVING

1 small head radicchio, leaves separated

Fresh mint leaves

Lemon wedges

In a large bowl, combine the ground beef, ground lamb, onion, garlic, tomato paste, parsley, mint, sumac, turmeric, cumin, salt and Aleppo pepper. Using your hands, form the mixture into oval-shaped, tablespoon-sized (15-g) meatballs. Heat a wide Dutch oven over medium-high heat, and drizzle with the olive oil. Place the kofta in the hot oil, and sear until a deep crust is formed, 3 to 4 minutes per side, or until just cooked through.

Once the kofta are done, make the quick tzatziki. In a small bowl, add the yogurt, cucumber, parsley, mint, lemon juice and salt, and mix together until well combined.

To assemble, place 1 kofta in a radicchio cup, and top with a dollop of tzatziki. Garnish with fresh mint, and serve with lemon wedges.

 TIP: Radicchio can have a bitter bite to it, so if you prefer something milder, use fresh butter lettuce or crisp romaine leaves.

TURKISH BEEF STEW WITH WHITE BEANS

YIELDS
4
servings

Fasulye translates to "beans" in Turkish, and depending on where you go, you'll often find different styles of fasulye, such as a green beans and tomatoes (page 96) or, in this case, a hearty stew made with white beans. The rich flavors come from the seasoned meat that infuses the rest of the layers in the dish, and canned beans provide a much faster overall cook time.

Serve with Zucchini and Herb Pilaf (page 135) and Turkish Shepherd's Salad with Fresh Herbs and Sumac (page 160) on the side.

1½ lb (680 g) beef stew meat, cut into chunks

1 tsp paprika

1 tsp cumin

1 tsp kosher salt

½ tsp coriander

½ tsp black pepper

2 tbsp (30 ml) olive oil

1 shallot, diced

3 cloves garlic, finely chopped

2 tbsp (32 g) tomato paste

1 medium vine-ripened tomato, diced

1 Anaheim or green bell pepper, seeds removed, cut into ½-inch (1.3-cm) chunks

3 cups (720 ml) low-sodium chicken stock, divided

1 (15.5-oz [439-g]) can white beans, drained and rinsed

Chopped fresh parsley leaves or dill, for garnish

Pat the beef dry with paper towels, and set aside. In a small bowl, combine the paprika, cumin, salt, coriander and pepper. Season the cubed meat with the spice mixture so all the sides are evenly coated.

Heat a wide Dutch oven over medium-high heat, and add the olive oil. In batches, add the seasoned meat, and sear on all sides until a deep crust forms, 2 to 3 minutes, and turning as needed, then remove to a plate and set aside.

Add the shallot, and sauté until lightly caramelized, 2 to 3 minutes. Stir in the garlic, and sauté for another minute. Stir in the tomato paste, using a spatula to break up the paste into the residual oil. Add the tomato and Anaheim pepper, and sauté for another 2 to 3 minutes so the tomato releases its juices.

Pour in ½ cup (120 ml) of the chicken stock, and use the spatula to scrape any bits from the bottom of the Dutch oven. Add in the white beans and seared meat with any accumulated juices, along with the remaining chicken stock. Cover with a lid, and bring the stew to a boil. Reduce the heat to a constant simmer, and cook for 1 to 1½ hours, until the meat is incredibly tender and the sauce has thickened slightly.

To serve, ladle the fasulye into bowls, and garnish with parsley or dill.

TIP: If you prefer dried beans, soak ½ cup (90 g) of dried white or cannellini beans in a large bowl of water for at least 8 hours. Before starting the stew, boil the soaked beans for 40 minutes until softened, then follow the rest of the recipe.

CINNAMON-SPICED RICE WITH LAMB AND ALMONDS (KABSA)

YIELDS
4 to 6
servings

When we lived in Southern California, there was a dish called kabsa I would always order at a local Lebanese restaurant. Unfortunately, I was never able to secure the specifics of the recipe, but I took to my taste buds and spice drawer to figure out the closest possibilities.

This is my humble take on that fantastic dish. Chunks of lamb are generously seasoned with a handful of spices, creating an intense depth of flavor. Other aromatics include a bay leaf and a cinnamon stick, and the addition of savory bell pepper and sweet dried fruit presents some striking flavors.

2 lb (907 g) lamb shoulder, cut into 1-inch (2.5-cm) cubes

1 tsp cumin

1 tsp turmeric

½ tsp coriander

¼ tsp ground cinnamon

½ tsp kosher salt

¼ tsp ground black pepper

2 tbsp (30 ml) ghee

1 small yellow onion, thinly sliced

1 green bell pepper, seeds removed, diced

2 cloves garlic, minced

2 tbsp (32 g) tomato paste

1 cup (200 g) uncooked basmati rice, rinsed well

2½ cups (600 ml) chicken stock

1 bay leaf

1 cinnamon stick

1 cup (150 g) dried apricots, roughly chopped

¼ cup (35 g) toasted pine nuts, plus more for garnish

¼ cup (27 g) toasted slivered almonds, plus more for garnish

Chopped fresh parsley leaves, for garnish

Preheat the oven to 350°F (176°C). Season the lamb with the cumin, turmeric, coriander, cinnamon, salt and pepper, making sure that all sides of the meat are evenly coated with the spices.

Meanwhile, heat a Dutch oven over high heat, and add the ghee. Once the ghee melts, sear the cubed lamb until all the pieces are deeply caramelized on all sides, 2 to 3 minutes per side. Reduce the heat to medium, cover with a lid and continue cooking the lamb for 10 minutes. Transfer the lamb to a plate and set aside.

Add the onion and bell pepper, and sauté for 3 to 5 minutes, until the vegetables begin to soften. Stir in the garlic, and sauté for another minute. Stir in the tomato paste, and cook for another 2 to 3 minutes, giving the paste a chance to break down into the oil and other aromatics. Stir the basmati rice into the flavored oil, and sauté for another 30 seconds, so all of the grains are coated with the flavored oil.

Pour in the chicken stock, using a spatula to scrape up any meaty bits from the bottom of the Dutch oven, and spread the rice out into an even layer. Return the lamb and any accumulated juices to the pan. Spread the lamb into an even layer among the rice. Nestle the bay leaf and cinnamon stick into the liquid, and scatter the dried apricots, pine nuts and almonds around the rice and lamb.

Bring up to a simmer, and once simmering, cover the Dutch oven and place it in the oven. Cook for 20 to 25 minutes, until the liquid has absorbed and the lamb is tender. Once done, remove from the oven, and let it cool for at least 10 minutes.

Before serving, remove the bay leaf and cinnamon stick, and use a fork to fluff the rice. Garnish the kabsa with chopped parsley and additional toasted nuts.

MOROCCAN MEATBALLS WITH SAFFRON COUSCOUS

YIELDS
4
servings

Intensely flavored meatballs are seasoned with bold spices of turmeric, coriander and just a touch of cinnamon, inspired by Moroccan flavors. Once the meatballs are browned, other aromatics are added for the saffron couscous. Couscous is a fantastic addition to one-pot recipes because it cooks in just about the time needed to boil water. Leave the lid on for a few minutes so the couscous can soak up the stock, and the finished product is incredibly fluffy and fragrant. This is fantastic served alongside a Cucumber Yogurt Salad (page 143) and a dollop of harissa.

MEATBALL MIXTURE

½ lb (226 g) ground beef

½ lb (226 g) ground lamb

1 egg

½ white or yellow onion, diced

2 cloves garlic, grated or minced

1½ tsp (3 g) cumin

1 tsp paprika

¾ tsp turmeric

¾ tsp coriander

¼ tsp ground cinnamon

¾ tsp kosher salt

¼ tsp black pepper

⅓ cup (18 g) panko bread crumbs

¼ cup (4 g) chopped fresh cilantro leaves

2 tbsp (30 ml) olive oil

SAFFRON COUSCOUS

½ white or yellow onion, diced

2 cloves garlic, finely chopped

1½ cup (360 ml) chicken stock

Pinch of saffron

1 cup (173 g) dry couscous

1 cup (150 g) dried apricots or dried figs, diced

Pomegranate seeds, for garnish

Chopped fresh cilantro leaves, for garnish

For the meatballs, in a large bowl, add the ground beef, ground lamb, egg, onion, garlic, cumin, paprika, turmeric, coriander, cinnamon, salt, pepper, bread crumbs and cilantro. Mix well to combine. Using your hands, form the mixture into tablespoon-sized (15-g) meatballs and set aside.

In a wide Dutch oven over medium-high heat, add the olive oil, and sear the meatballs until deeply brown on all sides and cooked throughout, 4 to 5 minutes per side. Remove and set aside.

For the couscous, in the same Dutch oven, add the onion, and sauté for 2 to 3 minutes, until the onion is softened but not caramelized. Stir in the garlic, and sauté for another minute. Pour in the chicken stock, and add a pinch of saffron, crushing the threads between your fingers. Bring the liquid to a boil. Once boiling, stir in the couscous, and nestle the meatballs into the couscous, along with the dried apricots.

Turn off the heat, and cover the Dutch oven. Cook for 10 minutes, until the couscous is cooked through and tender. Once done, fluff the couscous with a fork, and garnish with pomegranate seeds and cilantro.

STUFFED GRAPE LEAVES WITH GROUND BEEF, HERBS AND DRIED FRUIT

YIELDS
8 to 10
servings

There is nothing like my mom's classic stuffed grape leaves, which was one of the first recipes I learned to make. My family's version is made very simply, where the grape leaves are only stuffed with ground beef and rice. Over the years, I've played around with the fillings and modernized it a bit to include sweet golden raisins and loads of fresh herbs, giving the otherwise simple filling a slightly sweet and savory combination.

1 jar (about 40) grape leaves in brine

1 lb (454 g) ground beef

¾ cup (150 g) uncooked Jasmine rice, rinsed well

½ cup (30 g) finely chopped fresh parsley leaves

½ cup (30 g) finely chopped fresh dill

3 bunches green onions, finely chopped

½ cup (73 g) golden raisins, roughly chopped, plus ¼ cup (37 g) whole golden raisins

1 lemon, zested and thinly sliced

1 tsp kosher salt

1 tsp Aleppo pepper

1 tsp cumin

2 cups (480 ml) vegetable or chicken stock

Remove the grape leaves from the jar and rinse them under cool water, separating each leaf. Pat the leaves dry and set aside.

In a large bowl, add the ground beef, Jasmine rice, parsley, dill, green onions, chopped golden raisins, lemon zest, salt, Aleppo pepper and cumin. Give everything a good mix so all of the herbs and spices are evenly incorporated into the meat.

Lay out one grape leaf, shiny side down, and cut off the hard stem with a paring knife. Place a tablespoon (15 g) of the meat mixture toward the bottom of the leaf. Begin to roll halfway, fold in the sides and then continue rolling until the leaf is rolled into a small package.

If there are any broken leaves, lay those at the bottom of a wide Dutch oven, and place the rolled grape leaves, seam side down, into the Dutch oven. Continue rolling the grape leaves until all of the mixture is used up, making sure the grape rolls are nestled together closely in the Dutch oven.

Pour the stock all around the grape leaves, and scatter the whole golden raisins over the top. Place the lemon slices in between the grape leaf rolls. Place the Dutch oven over medium heat, and bring to a simmer. Simmer the stuffed grape leaves for 1 hour or until the meat and rice is cooked through and tender and the liquid has absorbed.

Once done, allow the grape leaves to cool for at least 10 minutes and serve warm.

 TIP: If you don't have or like golden raisins and still want the sweet and savory combination, substitute with dried apricots, dried currants or dried cranberries.

BRACIOLE STUFFED WITH PINE NUTS AND PARMESAN

YIELDS
4 to 6
servings

Braciole is a braised meat recipe rolled up and stuffed with various fillings. I've seen all sorts of fillings, from simple bread crumbs and cheese to dried fruits or even a hard-boiled egg. This is one of those recipes to make on a weekend evening and let it simmer low and slow. The smell is intoxicating, and the infused sauce is even better the next day. Serve alongside Creamy Mascarpone Polenta (page 120) for a delicious, comforting meal.

BRACIOLE

2 lb (907 g) flank steak

Kosher salt and ground black pepper, for seasoning

¼ cup (14 g) panko bread crumbs

¼ cup (35 g) toasted pine nuts

¼ cup (25 g) grated Parmesan cheese

Zest of 1 lemon

¼ cup (15 g) finely chopped fresh parsley leaves

3 to 4 sprigs fresh thyme, leaves removed and chopped

3 to 4 sprigs fresh oregano, leaves removed and chopped

5 tbsp (75 ml) olive oil, divided

MARINARA SAUCE

½ onion, chopped

2 cloves garlic, finely chopped

2 tsp (2 g) dried oregano

½ tsp red pepper flakes

½ cup (120 ml) red wine, such as Cabernet Sauvignon

1 (32-oz [907-g]) can crushed tomatoes

½ tsp kosher salt

Chopped fresh parsley or basil leaves, for garnish

Lay the flank steak between two sheets of plastic wrap, and pound the steak with a meat mallet or meat tenderizer until it's an even and thin thickness. Season the steak evenly with salt and pepper on both sides.

In a medium bowl, combine the bread crumbs, pine nuts, Parmesan, lemon zest, parsley, thyme and oregano. Stir to combine so everything is mixed well, and add 2 tablespoons (30 ml) of olive oil to evenly coat the bread crumb mixture. Spread the filling evenly over the steak, and roll up the longer side of the steak until it's a tight roll. Tie the rolled flank steak with several pieces of butcher's twine so it's an even thickness.

Heat a wide Dutch oven to medium-high heat, and add 3 tablespoons (45 ml) of olive oil. Sear the braciole on all sides until it is deeply caramelized. Remove and set aside. Add the onion, and sauté for 3 to 4 minutes, until lightly caramelized. Add the garlic, oregano and red pepper flakes, and continue sautéing for another minute. Pour in the red wine and deglaze, using a spatula to scrape off any meaty bits from the bottom of the Dutch oven.

Pour in the crushed tomatoes. Fill the can halfway with water, and pour that into the sauce. Give everything a good mix, season with the salt and nestle the braciole and any accumulated juices into the tomato sauce. Cover the Dutch oven, leaving a small opening, and bring up to a boil. Then reduce to a simmer. Continue simmering for 1 to 1½ hours, until the meat is incredibly tender and the sauce has reduced slightly.

When ready to serve, remove the braciole from the marinara, and let it cool for at least 5 minutes. Cut off the butcher's twine, and discard. Slice the braciole into thick slices. Serve the sliced braciole on top of the marinara, and garnish with parsley or basil.

MOUSSAKA STEW WITH POTATOES AND ZUCCHINI

YIELDS
4 to 6
servings

Moussaka is a traditional Greek casserole with fried eggplant, zucchini and tomatoes, as well as layers of rich bechamel and meat sauce. It is worth the effort, but it is certainly not easy to create using one pot. Here I channeled the flavors of a moussaka and made a rustic and hearty beef stew. Once the beef stew is rich and condensed, a dollop of creamy and tangy labneh cheese is added at the very end, which takes inspiration from bechamel sauce without the heaviness or labor. This is the perfect stew to make on a cooler night when you are craving something comforting and satisfying.

Serve with toasted pita bread to sop up the delicious, beefy broth.

1½ to 2 lb (680 g to 907 g) beef stew meat, cubed

1 tsp paprika

¾ tsp kosher salt

½ tsp ground black pepper

½ tsp cumin

¼ tsp ground cinnamon

3 tbsp (45 ml) olive oil

½ red onion, diced

2 cloves garlic, finely chopped

2 tbsp (32 g) tomato paste

½ cup (120 ml) red wine, such as Cabernet Sauvignon

1 cup (150 g) thin-skinned potatoes, cut in half or quarters

1 small eggplant, peeled and cut into 1-inch (2.5-cm) cubes

3½ to 4 cups (840 ml to 960 ml) low-sodium beef stock

2 sprigs fresh oregano

1 bay leaf

1 zucchini, cut into ½-inch (1.3-cm) cubes

FOR SERVING

Labneh

Grated Parmesan cheese

Chopped fresh oregano or parsley leaves

Pat the cubed beef dry with paper towels, and season the meat with paprika, salt, pepper, cumin and cinnamon, making sure the spices are evenly coated all over the meat.

Heat a Dutch oven over medium-high heat, and add the olive oil. Once the oil is hot, sear the cubed meat in batches, until a deep crust forms, 3 to 4 minutes per side, then transfer to a plate and set aside.

Add the onion, and sauté for 4 to 5 minutes, until softened and translucent. Stir in the garlic, sautéing for another minute. Add the tomato paste, using a spatula to break up the tomato paste into the oil, and pour in the red wine, scraping up any residual meaty bits on the bottom.

To the same Dutch oven, add the potatoes and eggplant, and give everything a good stir so all the flavors begin to coat the vegetables. Return the cubed beef and any accumulated juices to the pan, and pour in the beef stock, just enough to cover all the vegetables. Nestle the oregano and bay leaf into the stew, and cover with a lid, leaving a small opening. Simmer the stew for 40 to 45 minutes, then add the zucchini, and continue simmering for another 10 to 15 minutes, until the meat and vegetables are cooked through and tender.

Before serving, remove the oregano sprigs and bay leaf, and discard. Ladle the stew into wide bowls, and garnish with a dollop of creamy labneh cheese, grated Parmesan cheese and more fresh oregano or parsley.

 TIP: Labneh cheese is a strained yogurt cheese that is very popular in Mediterranean cuisine. If you can't find labneh cheese, use thick full-fat plain Greek yogurt.

CHAPTER 3

FRESH AND FRAGRANT SEAFOOD RECIPES

When I want a quick and fresh dinner, fish and shellfish are the proteins I gravitate toward. I am so lucky to live in the Pacific Northwest and have access to such amazing seafood.

Here are a few tips for cooking fish. First, it should smell briny, like the ocean, and should not have any unpleasant odors. When looking for seafood, look for firm flesh that doesn't have any blemishes, bruising or additives. And just like other proteins, dry the fish well before seasoning and cooking. This helps the seasonings hold onto the fish and also results in a better sear.

A fish spatula is a great tool to use. It is flexible and thin enough to get under the fillet. As soon as your fish is opaque or has a nice golden color, flip it over and continue cooking the same way. Most fish fillets and shellfish don't need any more than 8 to 10 minutes of cooking time.

Instead of searing, you can also simmer fish in a flavorful broth, such as the Saucy Moroccan Fish with Peppers and Paprika (page 82). And during the summer months when cherry tomatoes are at their peak, try the Seared Halibut with Cherry Tomatoes and Summer Squash (page 70) for a light and flavorful weeknight dinner.

A frozen bag of wild-caught shrimp is perfect for those quick dinner nights and something that we always have on hand in the freezer for quick meals. The Greek-Inspired Shrimp with Olives, Tomatoes and Feta (page 74) is a perfect example of a recipe that was created for an impressive and easy dinner.

SHEET PAN SALMON SHAWARMA

YIELDS
4
servings

Inspired from the bold flavors of chicken shawarma, this salmon shawarma uses the same intense seasonings to create a fantastic weeknight recipe. The aromatic mixture has warm and smoky flavors, thanks to the earthy cumin and smoked paprika, and welcomes a splash of bright acidity from the fresh lemon juice. If salmon isn't available, this spiced mixture works with other types of fish, such as Arctic char and halibut, as well as shrimp.

Serve the salmon shawarma with a Spicy Chopped Tomato Salad with Pomegranate (page 151) or Cucumber Yogurt Salad with Mint and Pistachios (page 143) to balance the deep flavors.

1 to 1½ lb (454 g to 680 g) salmon fillet, bones removed

¼ cup (60 ml) olive oil

1 tbsp (15 ml) lemon juice

1 clove garlic, minced or grated

1 tsp kosher salt

¾ tsp turmeric

¾ tsp smoked paprika

¾ tsp cumin

Lemon wedges, for serving

Chopped fresh cilantro or parsley leaves, for garnish

Preheat the oven to 425°F (218°C). Dry the salmon fillet very well with paper towels; this will help the marinade stick to the fish easily. Place the salmon on a parchment paper–lined baking sheet.

In a small bowl, whisk the olive oil, lemon juice, garlic, salt, turmeric, smoked paprika and cumin together, and brush the mixture onto the salmon, making sure the entire fillet is evenly coated with the marinade.

Roast the salmon for 10 to 12 minutes, until just cooked through. For a crispy exterior, place the salmon under the broiler for an additional 1 to 2 minutes, if desired.

Once done, let the salmon cool slightly, and garnish with lemon wedges and cilantro or parsley.

 TIP: Thicker salmon fillets such as King salmon may take a few more minutes to cook, and likewise, a thinner cut such as sockeye salmon may need a few less minutes, so keep an eye on the doneness.

SPRING COD WITH LEEKS AND FAVA BEANS

YIELDS
2 to 4
servings

Fava beans, also called broad beans, are used throughout Mediterranean cooking and are one of the oldest protein sources in Middle Eastern cuisine. You'll often find fresh fava beans at the start of the spring season along with tender spring leeks. If using fresh fava beans, remove the beans from the thick pod, and give them a quick rinse. Then add the beans to boiling water for 1 minute until the beans turn bright green.

For a complete meal, serve alongside One-Pot Mujadara with Crispy Leeks (Labenese Rice and Lentils; page 124) or Baked Risotto with Spinach and Feta (page 119).

2 (6-oz [170-g]) cod fillets

1 tsp kosher salt

½ tsp ground black pepper

2 tbsp (30 ml) olive oil

2 tbsp (30 g) unsalted butter or ghee

1 leek, white and light green parts only, thinly sliced

2 cloves garlic, minced

1 tsp lemon zest

1 tbsp (15 ml) lemon juice

½ cup (120 ml) white wine, such as Pinot Grigio

1 cup (170 g) cooked frozen or cooked fresh fava beans

Chopped fresh parsley leaves, for garnish

Fresh basil leaves, for garnish

Season the cod fillets with salt and pepper on both sides, and set aside. Heat a wide Dutch oven over medium heat, and add the olive oil and butter. Once the butter is melted, add the leek, and sauté until it is very soft but not caramelized, 6 to 8 minutes. Stir the garlic in and sauté for another minute.

Stir in the lemon zest and juice, and pour in the white wine. Give everything a good stir, and let the wine reduce slightly for another minute. Add the fava beans, and continue sautéing for another minute, coating the fava beans with the flavored oil.

Place the cod fillets on top of the leek mixture, and use a spoon to baste any reserved sauce onto the fish. Cover the Dutch oven with a lid, and cook the cod for 6 to 8 minutes, until the fillets are just cooked through.

Garnish with the parsley and basil, and serve immediately.

TIPS: Fava beans freeze very well, and you can often find frozen fava beans in many grocery stores. But during the spring season, take advantage of the fresh broad beans and do the quick prep yourself. Then place the cooked fava beans in a resealable bag to freeze and use throughout the year.

If fava beans are not available, look for lima beans, which provide a similar flavor and texture.

PAPRIKA RICE WITH SHRIMP, ZUCCHINI AND OLIVES

YIELDS
4
servings

This dish is inspired by the bold flavors of Spanish paella but with a fraction of the effort. Typically, paella is made using a paella pan, which can take a bit more labor because the paella pan needs to be turned to ensure even cooking. Instead, we're taking advantage of the even cooking that an enameled Dutch oven offers and creating an incredibly fragrant and zesty one-pot rice dish.

There is a good kick of spice in this dish, thanks to the addition of a Fresno chile. If you prefer less or no spice, remove the seeds from the chile, or omit it all together.

1 lb (454 g) medium shrimp, peeled, deveined and tails removed

1 tsp kosher salt, divided

½ tsp ground black pepper

2 tbsp (30 ml) olive oil or avocado oil

½ white onion, diced

1 small Fresno or serrano chile, minced

3 cloves garlic, minced

1 tbsp (16 g) tomato paste

1 tsp smoked paprika

½ tsp ground coriander

Pinch of saffron

1 cup (200 g) basmati rice, rinsed

2 vine tomatoes, diced

2 cups (480 ml) low-sodium chicken stock

1 roasted bell pepper, cut into thin strips

1 cup (180 g) pitted and chopped Castelvetrano olives

1 zucchini, chopped into ½-inch (1.3-cm) pieces

Chopped fresh parsley leaves, for garnish

Lemon wedges, for garnish

In a large bowl, season the shrimp with ½ teaspoon of the kosher salt and the black pepper, and toss to combine and set aside.

Heat a wide Dutch oven over medium-high, and add the olive oil. Add the onion, and sauté for 3 to 4 minutes, until the onion is softened but not caramelized. Add the chile and garlic, and continue sautéing for another minute, until the garlic is fragrant. Stir in the tomato paste, using a spatula to break up the tomato paste so it melts into the oil. Add the smoked paprika, coriander, saffron and the remaining salt. Stir the rice into the Dutch oven, and give it a good mix so all of the grains are coated with the aromatic oil. Add the tomatoes, and continue sautéing for another 1 to 2 minutes, until the tomatoes begin to soften. Use the back of a spatula to spread the rice mixture into an even layer.

Pour in the chicken stock, and scatter the bell pepper, olives and zucchini on top of the rice. Cover the Dutch oven with a lid, and simmer for 20 minutes, until the rice is cooked through and the zucchini is just tender. Nestle the shrimp on top of the rice mixture, and cook, covered, for another 5 to 6 minutes, until the shrimp are just cooked through.

To serve, garnish with parsley and lemon wedges.

SEARED HALIBUT WITH CHERRY TOMATOES AND SUMMER SQUASH

Living in the Pacific Northwest, we are lucky to have bountiful seafood around us. And when seafood is this delicious and summer's produce is at its peak, there is not much doctoring that needs to be done.

YIELDS
2
servings

This is a simple seafood recipe that we have on rotation. I highly recommend waiting until summer's cherry tomatoes are in season, though a good substitute would be sun-dried tomatoes, which will be more savory compared to sweet summer tomatoes.

Serve the seared halibut with Creamy Mascarpone Polenta (page 120) or a fresh salad, such as Citrus Fennel Salad with Orange Blossom Vinaigrette (page 147), for a lovely summer dinner.

2 (4- to 6-oz [113- to 170-g]) halibut fillets, or other firm white fish

1 tsp kosher salt, plus more as needed

½ tsp ground black pepper

2 tbsp (30 ml) olive oil

2 cloves garlic, thinly sliced

1 yellow summer squash, cut into small chunks

1 pint (298 g) cherry tomatoes, larger ones cut in half

Zest of ½ lemon

½ cup (120 ml) dry white wine, such as Pinot Grigio

1 tbsp (15 g) unsalted butter

4 to 5 fresh basil leaves, for garnish

Season the halibut with salt and pepper on both sides. Heat a wide Dutch oven over medium heat, and add the olive oil. As soon as the oil is just shimmering, sear the halibut until lightly golden brown, 3 to 4 minutes per side. Once the halibut is cooked, remove and keep warm.

Reduce the heat to medium, add the garlic and sauté for 30 seconds to a minute, until the garlic is fragrant but not caramelized in color. Add the yellow squash, cherry tomatoes and lemon zest, and season the vegetables with salt. Give everything a stir, and sauté for 3 to 4 minutes so the tomatoes begin to soften.

Pour in the wine, and use a spatula to scrape any remaining bits left on the bottom of the Dutch oven. Add the butter, and continue sautéing until the butter is melted. As the tomatoes cook, use the back of the spatula to press onto the cherry tomatoes, releasing their juices, for another 30 seconds.

To serve, spoon the tomato–zucchini mixture around the seared halibut, along with any accumulated sauce. Garnish with basil, and serve immediately.

STEAMED MUSSELS WITH PEARL COUSCOUS AND SAFFRON

YIELDS
4
servings

Each year on my birthday, I have one request: to eat a big bowl of steamed mussels with copious amounts of crusty bread. If it's not mussels, it's always steamed clams (page 78).

This twist on classic steamed mussels cooks with chewy pearl couscous and aromatic saffron. The broth is infused with a sweet tomato, aromatic saffron and wine mixture and begs for some crusty bread for dipping. Serve these steamed mussels alongside Citrus Fennel Salad with Orange Blossom Vinaigrette (page 147). The combination would be a delightful pairing.

Pinch of saffron

2 tbsp (30 ml) warm water

2 tbsp (30 ml) olive oil

1 shallot, thinly sliced

½ fennel bulb, thinly sliced

2 cloves garlic, finely chopped

1 medium tomato, diced

½ cup (120 ml) white wine, such as Pinot Grigio

¼ tsp kosher salt

2 cups (480 ml) low-sodium vegetable stock

1 cup (170 g) dried pearl couscous

2 lb (907 g) mussels, cleaned

1 tbsp (15 ml) lemon juice

Chopped fresh mint, cilantro or oregano leaves, for garnish

Lemon wedges, for serving

In a small bowl, steep the saffron in the warm water for about 10 minutes. Meanwhile, in a deep Dutch oven over medium-high heat, add the olive oil. Add the shallot and fennel, and sauté until the fennel has softened, 5 to 6 minutes. Add the garlic, and sauté for another minute.

Add the tomato with any accumulated juices, and pour in the white wine and saffron liquid. Give everything a stir, and season with salt. Continue simmering for another 2 to 3 minutes, until the tomato softens and releases its juices.

Pour in the vegetable stock and couscous, and give everything a good stir. Cover, and cook the couscous for 5 to 7 minutes. Add the mussels, gently stirring them into the liquid. Cover and continue cooking until the mussels open up, 6 to 8 minutes more.

At this point, the couscous should be cooked through and tender, and the mussels will have opened up. Discard any mussels that have not opened, and stir in the lemon juice. Remove the Dutch oven from the heat, and ladle the mussels and couscous into wide bowls. Garnish with mint, and serve with lemon wedges.

TIP: Like clams, mussels should be bought fresh and preferably used the same day. Mussels do take some time to clean, but it is worth it to not bite into something undesirable. To clean mussels, use a towel to pull off the "beard" that is attached to the mussel. Then, 20 to 30 minutes before cooking, place the mussels in ice cold water, and add a pinch of salt or flour to the water to help the mussels spit out any debris.

GREEK-INSPIRED SHRIMP WITH OLIVES, TOMATOES AND FETA

YIELDS
4
servings

Whenever I need a quick and flavorful meal, I turn to a bag of frozen shrimp. Shrimp defrosts very quickly, cooks fast and is able to take on a multitude of flavors. Here, simple sautéed shrimp are flavored with classic Greek ingredients and would be perfect to serve alongside Zucchini and Herb Pilaf (page 135) or Greek-Inspired Panzanella with Red Wine Vinaigrette and Feta (page 156).

3 tbsp (45 ml) olive oil

1 shallot, finely chopped

3 cloves garlic, finely chopped

½ tsp dried oregano

2 medium tomatoes, diced

1 lb (454 g) medium shrimp, peeled and deveined

½ tsp kosher salt

¼ tsp ground black pepper

¼ cup (60 ml) dry white wine, such as Pinot Grigio

½ cup (90 g) chopped Kalamata olives

½ lemon, zested and juiced

FOR SERVING

4 oz (113 g) feta cheese, roughly crumbled

Fresh mint, cilantro and/or oregano

Lemon wedges

Heat a wide Dutch oven over medium heat, and add the olive oil. Add the shallot, and sauté until softened but not caramelized, 3 to 4 minutes. Add the garlic and oregano, and sauté for another minute. Stir in the tomatoes with any accumulated juices, and cook for 2 to 3 minutes, until the tomatoes begin to soften.

Add the shrimp, and season everything with salt and pepper. Cook the shrimp until they are opaque and just cooked through, 4 to 5 minutes. Pour in the wine, and stir everything together until the wine reduces, creating a sauce.

Turn the heat off, add the Kalamata olives, lemon zest and juice and stir once more. Garnish the shrimp with crumbled feta and fresh herbs, and serve with lemon wedges.

LEMONY SHRIMP WITH ORZO AND ASPARAGUS

Simple and fresh, this recipe comes together in nearly 30 minutes from start to finish, thanks to quick-cooking shrimp and asparagus. Thicker asparagus spears may take a minute longer to cook but have a short window of being perfectly tender to being overcooked.

1 lb (454 g) medium shrimp, peeled, deveined and tails removed

3 cloves garlic, finely chopped, divided

3 tbsp (45 ml) olive oil, divided

Zest of ½ lemon

¼ tsp salt

Ground black pepper

1 small shallot, finely chopped

1½ cups (170 g) orzo

½ cup (120 ml) dry white wine, such as Pinot Grigio

3 cups (720 ml) chicken stock

Juice of ½ lemon

1 bunch asparagus, ends trimmed and cut into 1-inch (2.5-cm) pieces

½ lemon, thinly sliced

4 oz (113 g) feta, roughly crumbled

Chopped fresh mint, parsley and/or cilantro leaves, for garnish

In a bowl, add the shrimp, 1 clove of garlic, 1 tablespoon (15 ml) of the olive oil, the lemon zest, salt and pepper, and toss to combine. Let the shrimp marinate for at least 10 minutes while you start the rest of the recipe.

Heat a wide Dutch oven over medium heat, and add the remaining olive oil. Add the shallot, and sauté for 2 to 3 minutes, until softened. Add the remaining garlic, and sauté for another minute. Stir in the orzo, making sure all of the grains are coated with the flavorful oil. Pour in the white wine, and continue cooking for another minute, until the wine reduces.

Pour in the chicken stock and lemon juice, and cover the Dutch oven with a lid, leaving a small opening. Bring the liquid to a boil, then reduce the heat to a simmer and cook for 7 to 8 minutes, until the orzo is almost cooked through.

Scatter the asparagus, lemon slices and shrimp on top of the orzo, and continue cooking for another 5 to 6 minutes, until the shrimp are just cooked through and the asparagus is bright and tender.

Once the orzo is cooked and the shrimp are tender, turn off the heat, and garnish with the crumbled feta cheese and a sprinkle of chopped herbs.

 TIP: To ensure the asparagus stay crisp and bright, you can also blanch the asparagus. Place chopped asparagus in boiling water, and boil until they turn bright green, 3 to 4 minutes, then immediately remove to a bowl filled with ice water to stop the cooking.

STEAMED CLAMS WITH PRESERVED LEMON CHERMOULA

YIELDS
4
servings

Chermoula is a North African sauce that is made with lots of fresh herbs, spices and preserved lemon. Here, I took inspiration from those flavors, and instead of blending a separate sauce, I added the base ingredients right into the steamed clams. Clams love fresh herbs and lemon, and they welcome the addition of floral saffron as well.

Pinch of saffron

1 tbsp (15 ml) warm water

3 tbsp (45 ml) olive oil

1 shallot, thinly sliced

2 cloves garlic, finely chopped

½ preserved lemon, seeds removed, finely chopped

½ cup (120 ml) dry white wine, such as Pinot Grigio

2 lb (907 g) fresh clams, cleaned

Small bunch fresh parsley, leaves roughly chopped

Small bunch fresh cilantro, leaves roughly chopped

In a small bowl, steep the saffron in the warm water for at least 5 minutes.

Place a medium-sized Dutch oven over medium heat, and add the olive oil. Add the shallot, and sauté for 2 minutes, just until the shallot begins to soften. Stir in the garlic, and sauté for another minute. Add the preserved lemon, white wine and saffron water, and give everything a good mix. Sauté for another 1 to 2 minutes.

Add the clams to the pot, and use a wide spoon to give everything a gentle mix. Cover and cook the clams until they just begin to open up, 6 to 7 minutes.

Once the clams are cooked and they have all opened, add the chopped herbs, and give everything one final stir. Serve the steamed clams in wide bowls with any accumulated juices.

TIP: Cleaning the clams takes longer than cooking them, but the effort is worth it to avoid biting into a piece of sand. To clean clams, scrub each clam with a soft brush, and soak the clams for 20 minutes in icy-cold water with a pinch of salt thrown in, which helps the clams spit out any sand.

HONEY-HARISSA SALMON WITH KALE AND CHICKPEAS

YIELDS
4
servings

Salmon is often our go-to dinner during the week. Maybe it's because we're lucky to be surrounded by fantastic wild salmon coming from Alaska, so we like to take full advantage of it and find creative ways to let the salmon shine.

Hot honey has been a trend lately, and for good reason, so we're taking a Mediterranean approach and whisking together spicy harissa paste with sweet honey. As the salmon cooks, the mixture caramelizes ever so slightly, creating a delicious and slightly sticky layer.

2 tbsp (30 ml) olive oil, plus more for drizzling

2 cloves garlic, finely chopped

2 bunches Dino or Lacinato kale, leaves removed and roughly chopped

1 (15.5-oz [439-g]) can chickpeas, drained and rinsed

½ tsp kosher salt

HONEY-HARISSA MARINADE

¼ cup (60 g) harissa paste

1 tbsp (15 ml) honey

½ tsp kosher salt

¼ tsp sumac

1 to 1½ lb (454 to 680 g) salmon fillets, at least ½ inch (1.3 cm) thick, bones removed

FOR SERVING

Pinch of Aleppo pepper

Lemon wedges

Preheat the oven to 400°F (204°C). Heat a wide Dutch oven over medium heat, and add the olive oil. Add the garlic, and sauté for 1 to 2 minutes, until just softened but not caramelized. Add the kale and chickpeas, and season with salt. Turn off the heat and set aside.

Next, make the marinade. In a small bowl, whisk the harissa paste, honey, salt and sumac together until well combined.

Nestle the salmon on top of the kale and chickpeas, and spoon the honey-harissa sauce over the fillets (saving some for serving, if desired), making sure there is an even, thin coating on the salmon flesh. Drizzle everything with extra olive oil. Roast the salmon for 10 to 12 minutes, until the salmon is just cooked through and the kale is tender.

Remove the salmon from the oven, and let it cool slightly before serving. Serve with Aleppo pepper and lemon wedges.

 TIP: Salmon cooks relatively quickly, so look for vegetables that complement the same cooking time. If you don't have kale, fresh arugula or even small cubes of zucchini would work well.

SAUCY MOROCCAN FISH WITH PEPPERS AND PAPRIKA

YIELDS
4 servings

Moroccan fish is a popular dish to make amongst Sephardic Jews during the Sabbath. Over the last few years, there have been some twists on the stew, where some have tomatoes or olives or use different types of fish, such as salmon. It is an easy-to-put-together stew with big, bold flavors of spicy harissa, warm paprika and earthy turmeric. And I highly recommend serving this with Vegetable Couscous with Za'atar and Golden Raisins (page 131) to soak up that delectable sauce.

SAUCE

3 tbsp (45 ml) olive oil

1 small yellow onion, thinly sliced

2 cloves garlic, finely chopped

2 red or orange bell peppers, thinly sliced

3 tbsp (48 g) tomato paste

1 tbsp (15 g) harissa paste

1 tsp turmeric

1 tsp paprika

½ tsp cumin

2 cups (480 ml) low-sodium vegetable stock

1 (15.5-oz [439-g]) can chickpeas, drained and rinsed

1 tbsp (15 ml) lemon juice

½ tsp kosher salt

COD

1 lb (454 g) cod fillets, or other firm white fish

1 tsp kosher salt

½ tsp ground black pepper

½ tsp turmeric

½ lemon, thinly sliced

Chopped fresh parsley or cilantro leaves, for garnish

Heat a Dutch oven over medium heat, and add the olive oil. Add the onion, and sauté until the onion is very soft but not too deeply caramelized, 6 to 8 minutes. Add the garlic, and sauté for another minute. Add the bell peppers, and sauté for another 2 minutes to soften the peppers. Stir in the tomato paste, harissa paste, turmeric, paprika and cumin, breaking down the tomato and harissa pastes so they begin to melt into the oil. Pour in the vegetable stock, chickpeas and lemon juice, and give everything a good stir. Season with kosher salt, and bring to a gentle simmer.

Meanwhile, season the cod fillets with salt, pepper and turmeric on all sides. Nestle the fish into the simmering sauce, and scatter the lemon slices on top of the stew. Spoon some of the sauce over the fish, and place a lid on, leaving a small opening.

Continue simmering until the fish is just cooked through, about 10 minutes. Remove the lid, and continue simmering for another 5 minutes to thicken the sauce. Once done, remove from the heat, and garnish the fish stew with parsley or cilantro. Serve immediately.

SEARED COD WITH RUSTIC ROMESCO SAUCE

YIELDS
4
servings

When we traveled to Barcelona a few years ago, one of the dishes I couldn't stop thinking about was cod with Romesco. A firm yet buttery white fish paired with the liveliest Romesco sauce, the dish hit every single taste bud. The combination of the sweet roasted peppers with savory toasted almonds and a hint of bright vinegar right at the end is extraordinary. I would even suggest making a double batch of the Romesco sauce to serve alongside grilled meats or as a spread for sandwiches.

ROMESCO SAUCE

1 jarred roasted bell pepper

5 to 6 sun-dried tomatoes in oil

1 clove garlic, roughly chopped

¼ cup (36 g) toasted almonds

2 tbsp (30 ml) olive oil, plus more for drizzling

½ tsp kosher salt

Pinch of cayenne

Water, as needed

1 to 2 dashes of red wine vinegar

COD

1- to 1½-lb (454-g to 680-g) cod fillets, or other firm white fish

½ tsp kosher salt

½ tsp ground black pepper

2 tbsp (30 ml) olive oil, plus more for garnish

Chopped fresh parsley leaves, for garnish

Lemon zest, for garnish

To make the Romesco sauce, in a food processor or blender, combine the roasted bell pepper, sun-dried tomatoes, garlic, almonds, olive oil, salt and cayenne, and pulse until well incorporated. If the mixture is too coarse, add 1 tablespoon (15 ml) of water at a time until you reach the desired consistency. The texture should be thick without any large pieces of almond leftover. Add a few dashes of red wine vinegar, and give the Romesco sauce one final pulse. Set aside.

Generously season the cod fillets with kosher salt and pepper on all sides. Heat a wide Dutch oven over medium-high heat, and add the olive oil. As soon as the oil begins to shimmer, add the cod fillets, and sear until a deep golden crust is formed, 3 to 4 minutes. Then turn the cod over, and sear the other side for another 2 to 3 minutes, until just cooked through. Once done, remove from the heat and keep warm.

Spread a generous layer of the Romesco sauce onto a serving platter, and top with the seared cod. Garnish with another drizzle of olive oil, parsley and lemon zest. Serve immediately.

TIP: This recipe utilizes easy-to-find jarred roasted peppers, but if you prefer to roast your own, place a red bell pepper under the broiler, and broil for 3 to 4 minutes per side until deeply charred on all sides. Then, once cool enough to handle, peel off the charred peel, exposing the tender roasted pepper flesh.

PISTACHIO-CRUSTED SALMON WITH LEMON AND BROCCOLINI

YIELDS
4
servings

This pistachio-crusted salmon is often in our dinner rotation because it is intensely flavorful and also makes for an impressive meal without a lot of work. I usually keep it simple during midweek, topping the salmon with pistachios, panko, herbs and lemon zest, but the addition of ground pistachio takes the crispy crust over the top. If you don't like pistachios, substitute with ground almonds or hazelnuts. And if you don't like nuts at all, omit and increase the panko by ¼ cup (14 g).

Broccolini is the more delicate and tender cousin of broccoli and, personally, one of my favorite vegetables. It cooks in mere minutes and makes for the perfect accompaniment to roasted fish, also cooking in the same amount of time.

PISTACHIO-CRUSTED SALMON

3 tbsp (45 ml) olive oil, divided

1 to 1½ lb (454 to 680 g) salmon fillets, at least ½ inch (1.3 cm) thick, bones removed

1 tsp kosher salt

½ tsp ground black pepper

2 tbsp (30 ml) Dijon mustard

¼ cup (25 g) finely chopped pistachios

⅓ cup (18 g) panko bread crumbs

1 tbsp (4 g) finely chopped fresh parsley leaves, plus more for garnish

1 tsp lemon zest

BROCCOLINI

1 bunch broccolini, thicker stems cut in half lengthwise

½ tsp kosher salt

¼ tsp ground black pepper

2 tbsp (30 ml) olive oil

Lemon wedges, for serving

Tzatziki, for serving (page 49; optional)

Preheat the oven to 425°F (218°C). On the bottom of a wide Dutch oven, brush 1 tablespoon (15 ml) of the olive oil; this will help prevent the salmon fillets from sticking.

Place the salmon, flesh side up, in the Dutch oven, and season the fillets with salt and pepper. Brush a thin layer of Dijon mustard onto each fillet.

In a small bowl, mix the pistachios, bread crumbs, the remaining 2 tablespoons (30 ml) of olive oil, parsley and lemon zest, and toss to combine, making sure the oil evenly coats all of the bread crumbs and pistachios. Top the salmon with the pistachio mixture, using your hands to gently press the mixture into the salmon flesh.

Arrange the broccolini around the salmon, and season the broccolini with salt, pepper and olive oil. Bake for 10 to 12 minutes, until the salmon is just cooked through and the broccolini is tender.

Once done, remove from the oven and garnish with parsley and serve with lemon wedges and tzatziki.

 TIP: Look for fillets of salmon that are closer to the belly, which will be thicker and have more fat and flavor.

CHAPTER 4

COLORFUL AND HEARTY VEGETABLE MAINS

Yes, vegetables can be the star of the show, and these filling vegetarian recipes prove that colorful vegetables can take on any meaty dish.

The Root Vegetable Tagine with Harissa and Preserved Lemon (page 91) may be one of my favorite recipes from this book. Chunks of sweet butternut squash simmer with bold flavors of harissa and preserved lemon. There is so much flavor packed in one pot; it'll look like you cooked for hours!

Dutch oven zaalouk (page 107) is inspired by the Moroccan tomato and eggplant salad, where tomatoes, eggplant and warm spices simmer together until the mixture forms a thick paste. Finish with a final squeeze of fresh lemon juice, and serve with lots of toasted pita for scooping up the smoky and savory paste.

For a quick tapas-inspired bite, try the Paprika and Garlic–Roasted Potatoes with Creamy Feta Sauce (page 100), which is inspired by the Spanish tapas dish patatas bravas. Chunks of potatoes are seasoned with condensed tomato paste and smoky paprika, creating a delicious blend of flavors. And the best part may be the cool and creamy feta sauce that is drizzled on top.

And for a comforting treat, the Smoky Vegetable Bean Stew with Broiled Halloumi (page 111) will have you craving vegetables every night of the week. Halloumi is able to hold up to high-heat cooking, and the halloumi cheese ever so gently caramelizes on top of the saucy vegetables, creating the most delicious cheesy topping.

ROOT VEGETABLE TAGINE WITH HARISSA AND PRESERVED LEMON

YIELDS
4 servings

Full of bold, pungent flavors, this modernized tagine recipe takes strong inspiration from the popular Moroccan stew. Tagine can be made in a number of ways, with different proteins such as fish or chicken and, in this case, a vegetarian version that utilizes hearty root vegetables that are able to hold up both the strong flavors and simmering time. Serve the vegetable tagine with Vegetable Couscous with Za'atar and Golden Raisins (page 131) for a truly spectacular, flavorful dinner.

Pinch of saffron

2 tbsp (30 ml) warm water

2 tbsp (30 ml) olive oil

1 shallot, thinly sliced

2 cloves garlic, minced

1 small jalapeño, minced, optional

1 tsp smoked paprika

1 tsp turmeric

½ tsp coriander

¼ tsp ground cinnamon

1 tbsp (15 g) harissa paste

1 small preserved lemon, seeds removed, finely chopped

1 small butternut squash, peeled and cut into 1-inch (2.5-cm) cubes

1 sweet potato, peeled and cut into 1-inch (2.5-cm) cubes

2 medium carrots, peeled and cut into ½-inch (1.3-cm) pieces

3 cups (720 ml) low-sodium vegetable stock

1 (15.5-oz [439-g]) can chickpeas, drained and rinsed

1 cup (180 g) whole Castelvetrano olives

1 cup (150 g) dried apricots, roughly chopped

Lemon wedges, for serving

Pomegranate seeds, for garnish

Chopped fresh parsley or cilantro leaves, for garnish

In a small bowl, steep the saffron in the warm water for at least 5 minutes.

Heat a tall Dutch oven over medium-high heat, and add the olive oil. Add the shallot, and sauté for 3 to 4 minutes just to soften. Stir in the garlic and jalapeño, and sauté for another minute. Stir the smoked paprika, turmeric, coriander and cinnamon into the oil for 30 seconds, waking up the spices. Add the harissa paste and preserved lemon, and stir so the harissa paste can gently melt into the other aromatics. Add the butternut squash, sweet potato, carrots and vegetable stock and stir.

Cover the Dutch oven, and simmer for about 20 minutes, until the vegetables are halfway cooked through. Then add the chickpeas, olives and dried apricots, and continue simmering for another 20 minutes, or until the vegetables are just fork-tender.

Once done, the sauce should have thickened slightly and the vegetables should be tender. Remove the tagine from the heat, garnish with a squeeze of lemon juice and top with the pomegranate seeds and parsley or cilantro.

ROASTED EGGPLANT WITH POMEGRANATE MOLASSES AND ZHUG VINAIGRETTE

YIELDS
4
servings

If you aren't familiar, zhug is a popular Yemenite hot sauce made up of lots of herbs and hot pepper. I took inspiration from the hot, herby sauce and turned it into a looser vinaigrette, which glides over the roasted eggplant beautifully. If you prefer less heat, omit the seeds in the chile; the vinaigrette will still have big flavors.

EGGPLANT

2 medium eggplants, cut in half lengthwise

Kosher salt

2 tbsp (30 ml) honey

1 tbsp (15 ml) pomegranate molasses

1 tbsp (15 ml) olive oil

ZHUG VINAIGRETTE

½ cup (30 g) chopped fresh parsley leaves

½ cup (50 g) chopped fresh mint leaves

½ cup (24 g) chopped fresh chives

1 small jalapeño, chopped

1 clove garlic, chopped

½ lemon, zested and juiced

½ tsp coriander

½ tsp cumin

¼ cup (60 ml) olive oil

½ tsp kosher salt

Water, as needed

TOPPINGS

Toasted pine nuts

Pomegranate seeds

Crumbled feta cheese

Aleppo pepper

Honey

Lemon wedges, for serving

Preheat the oven to 425°F (218°C), and line a baking sheet with parchment paper.

Cut cross-hatch slits into the flesh of the eggplants, and sprinkle the flesh with salt. Let the eggplants sit while the oven preheats.

Meanwhile, in a small bowl, whisk the honey, pomegranate molasses and olive oil together. When the oven is ready, wipe off the excess salt and moisture on the eggplants. Lay the eggplants on the prepared baking sheet, and brush them with the pomegranate mixture. Roast the eggplants for 45 minutes, until they are soft and slightly caramelized.

While the eggplants are roasting, make the zhug vinaigrette. In a small food processor or blender, combine the parsley, mint, chives, jalapeño, garlic, lemon zest and juice, coriander, cumin, olive oil and salt. Give the mixture a blend until well combined, and add a tablespoon (15 ml) of water at a time as needed to thin out the consistency. Set aside.

Once done, place the roasted eggplants on a platter, and spoon the zhug vinaigrette onto the eggplant flesh. Garnish with toasted pine nuts, pomegranate seeds, crumbled feta, a sprinkle of Aleppo pepper, an extra drizzle of honey, if desired, and serve with lemon wedges.

 TIP: Look for young, smooth and firm eggplants. The flesh should be shiny and smooth, and the younger eggplants will have far fewer seeds, creating a sweeter flavor.

HERBY RICE AND ALMOND-STUFFED ZUCCHINI

YIELDS
4 to 6
servings

Kousa is a popular Lebanese zucchini recipe that is often made during peak zucchini season. Typically, green zebra zucchini is hollowed out and stuffed with an aromatic mixture of meat and rice and simmered with other vegetables in a tomato broth.

My version is a bit simpler and utilizes all of the same vibrant flavors. Instead of including ground meat, this vegan zucchini stuffing is made with an aromatic rice mixture and toasted nuts for added texture and flavor.

4 green zucchini

¼ cup (35 g) dry bulgur

½ cup (120 ml) hot water

2 tbsp (30 ml) olive oil

½ small yellow onion, diced

2 cloves garlic, minced

½ cup (100 g) cooked basmati rice

¼ cup (27 g) toasted slivered almonds

2 tbsp (8 g) chopped fresh parsley leaves, plus more for garnish

1 tbsp (3 g) chopped fresh chives, plus more for garnish

½ tsp dried mint

1 tsp kosher salt, divided

2 cups (480 ml) vegetable stock

2 tbsp (32 g) tomato paste

Cut the ends off of the zucchini, and cut each zucchini in half lengthwise. Use a small spoon to scoop out the flesh of the zucchini, leaving a ¼-inch (6-mm) border.

In a small bowl, add the bulgur, and pour in the hot water, making sure all of the bulgur is submerged. Cover the bowl with a small plate or sheet of plastic wrap, and set aside for 15 minutes, until all of the liquid has absorbed.

Meanwhile, heat a wide Dutch oven over medium-high heat, and add the olive oil. Add the onion, and sauté until softened and translucent, but not caramelized, 5 to 6 minutes. Add in the garlic, and sauté for another minute, then remove the sautéed onion and garlic to a large bowl along with the soaked bulgur, basmati rice, toasted almonds, parsley, chives, mint and ½ teaspoon of the salt. Give everything a good mix, and stuff 1 to 2 tablespoons (15 g to 30 g) of filling into the hollowed-out zucchini.

Pour the vegetable stock into the Dutch oven, whisk in the tomato paste and season with the remaining salt. Place the stuffed zucchini into the tomato broth, filling side up, and cover the Dutch oven, leaving a small opening. Bring up to a simmer, and continue cooking until the zucchini are just tender and the sauce has reduced slightly, 10 to 15 minutes.

Once done, remove from the heat, and serve the stuffed zucchini in wide bowls along with tomato broth. Garnish with more chopped parsley or mint.

TIP: When prepping the zucchini, cut off a thin slice from the bottom of the zucchini so, when the zucchini are placed in the Dutch oven, they will be stable and not roll over.

TURKISH GREEN BEANS OVER LEMONY YOGURT

YIELDS
2 to 4
servings

Fasulye is one of the first recipes my mom taught me to make, and depending on what part of the world you go to, you'll see fasulye in different ways. Some fasulye is made with green beans stewed with tomatoes, which is similar to what I grew up on, and other versions utilize white beans in a brothy stew, similar to Turkish Beef Stew with White Beans (page 50).

This version shares the same love I have for green beans with tomatoes and is served over a bright and creamy yogurt sauce. The tangy yogurt with rich and savory stewed beans is a fabulous combination of textures and flavors.

2 tbsp (30 ml) olive oil

1 small yellow onion, diced

2 cloves garlic, finely chopped

2 tbsp (32 g) tomato paste

¼ tsp smoked paprika

¼ tsp sumac

⅛ tsp allspice

⅛ tsp ground cinnamon

2 medium vine tomatoes, cut into small cubes

½ tsp kosher salt

1 lb (454 g) green beans, ends trimmed

1 (15.5-oz [439-g]) can cannellini beans, drained and rinsed

¾ cup (180 ml) low-sodium vegetable stock

LEMON YOGURT

1 cup (240 ml) plain Greek yogurt

½ preserved lemon, seeds removed, chopped finely

1 tbsp (15 ml) olive oil, for garnish

Fresh mint leaves, finely chopped, for garnish

Aleppo pepper, for garnish

Heat the Dutch oven over medium heat, and add the olive oil. Add the onion, and sauté until translucent, 3 to 5 minutes. Add the garlic, and sauté for another minute. Stir in the tomato paste, smoked paprika, sumac, allspice and cinnamon, and sauté for another minute, until all the spices and the tomato paste are mixed into the oil evenly. Add the tomatoes with any accumulated juices, and season with the salt. Cover and cook, allowing the tomatoes to soften, 6 to 8 minutes.

Add the green beans and cannellini beans, and pour in the vegetable stock. Give everything a good mix, and continue cooking, covered, over medium heat for 20 to 25 minutes, or until the green beans are tender and the tomatoes incredibly soft.

Meanwhile, spread a layer of yogurt onto a platter, and scatter with the preserved lemon. Layer the stewed beans on top of the yogurt, and garnish with a drizzle of olive oil, chopped mint leaves and Aleppo pepper.

 TIP: Frozen green beans work very well for this recipe—just decrease the time by 10 minutes, and simmer until warmed through and still tender.

VEGETARIAN STUFFED CABBAGE ROLLS WITH AVGOLEMONO

Often you will find stuffed cabbage rolls filled with meat and rice, but these cabbage rolls are filled with an herbaceous mixture of rice, chickpeas and chopped tomato. Toward the end of cooking, the simmering broth is gently mixed with egg yolks and fresh lemon juice, creating a luxurious and bright sauce to drizzle over the cabbage rolls.

1 head green cabbage, softened

2 tbsp (30 ml) olive oil

½ white onion, diced

3 cloves garlic, finely chopped

1 medium tomato, diced

1 cup (200 g) uncooked basmati rice

1 (15.5-oz [439-g]) can chickpeas, drained, rinsed and roughly chopped

1 lemon, zested and juiced

¼ cup (15 g) chopped fresh dill

¼ cup (15 g) chopped fresh parsley leaves

¼ cup (25 g) chopped fresh mint leaves

½ cup (68 g) toasted pine nuts

1 tsp kosher salt, plus more for seasoning

½ tsp ground black pepper, plus more for seasoning

3½ to 4 cups (840 ml to 960 ml) vegetable stock

2 egg yolks

Fresh dill, for garnish

Lemon wedges, for garnish

Separate the leaves of the cabbage head, being careful not to tear any. Keep the larger leaves for rolling, and save the smaller ones to line the Dutch oven.

For the filling, in the bottom of a Dutch oven over medium heat, add the olive oil. Add the onion, and sauté for 5 to 8 minutes, until softened and lightly caramelized. Add the garlic, and sauté for another minute.

To a large bowl, add the sautéed onion and garlic, the tomato, basmati rice, chickpeas, lemon zest, dill, parsley, mint, pine nuts, salt and pepper, and give everything a good mix.

Line the bottom of the Dutch oven with any small or torn cabbage leaves. Lay out a large cabbage leaf, and use a paring knife to cut away the thick stem off each leaf. Fill the cabbage leaf with ¼ cup (71 g) of the rice mixture, and roll the cabbage, tucking in the sides and creating a tight roll. Continue rolling until all of the mixture is used up, and lay the cabbage rolls seam side down in the Dutch oven.

Pour enough vegetable stock to just cover the cabbage rolls and season with salt and pepper. Cover with the lid, place the Dutch oven on the stove and bring to a boil, then reduce down to a simmer and cook for 45 to 50 minutes, until the cabbage is tender and the rice is cooked through.

At the end of cooking, in a small bowl, whisk the egg yolks and lemon juice, and slowly stream in ½ cup (120 ml) of the hot stock to temper the eggs. Turn the heat off, and pour the lemon and egg mixture back into the simmering cabbage rolls, gently tipping the Dutch oven to distribute the sauce evenly.

Serve the cabbage rolls in wide bowls, and spoon the avgolemono on top. Garnish with fresh dill and lemon wedges.

 TIP: To soften cabbage leaves, you can place the whole cabbage into the freezer the day before cooking, then remove it and let it thaw a few hours before making the recipe.

PAPRIKA AND GARLIC–ROASTED POTATOES WITH CREAMY FETA SAUCE

YIELDS
2 to 4
servings

When we visited Spain a few years ago, one of our favorite tapas was *patatas bravas*: fried potatoes tossed in a savory tomato-based sauce and drizzled with a creamy aioli. I took inspiration from that dish and added a Mediterranean twist. Instead of frying potatoes, chunks of potatoes are tossed with smoky paprika and rich tomato paste and roasted until tender. The roasted potatoes are drizzled with a creamy whipped feta sauce, which is smooth and savory.

Serve alongside Dutch Oven Roast Chicken with Preserved Lemon Compound Butter (page 21).

ROASTED POTATOES

4 to 5 Yukon gold potatoes, cut into small cubes

2 tbsp (32 g) tomato paste

½ tsp smoked paprika

½ tsp cayenne

2 tbsp (30 ml) olive oil

½ tsp kosher salt

WHIPPED FETA

¼ cup (60 ml) full-fat Greek yogurt

½ cup (75 g) feta

Juice of ½ lemon

1 clove garlic, roughly chopped

1 tbsp (15 ml) olive oil

½ tsp kosher salt

Water, if needed to thin out consistency

FOR SERVING

Sumac

Crumbled feta

Chopped fresh cilantro

Lemon wedges

Preheat the oven to 425°F (218°C) and line a baking sheet with parchment paper. Lay the potatoes in an even single layer on the prepared baking sheet.

In a small bowl, whisk together the tomato paste, smoked paprika, cayenne, olive oil and salt, and pour over the potatoes. Toss the tomato mixture with the potatoes so the sauce is evenly coated all over the potatoes. Roast the potatoes for 25 minutes until tender and caramelized on the outside.

Meanwhile, make the whipped feta. In a small food processor, add the Greek yogurt, feta, lemon juice, garlic, olive oil and salt, and blend until smooth. If the mixture is too thick, add a tablespoon (15 ml) of water at a time until the sauce is a smooth and pourable consistency.

Serve the potatoes on a platter, and drizzle with the whipped feta. Garnish with sumac, crumbled feta, cilantro and lemon wedges.

WARM AND CREAMY CARROT SOUP WITH CORIANDER

YIELDS
4
servings

Sweet carrots are the star of this recipe, and when simmered with warm spices of cumin and coriander, this smooth carrot soup makes for a perfect fall meal. An immersion blender or stick blender is highly recommended. As soon as the carrots are incredibly tender, the soup can be blended to a silky smooth consistency in the same pot.

To contrast the warm and sweet notes of the soup, tangy pomegranate molasses and yogurt is drizzled on top, creating even more layers of bold flavors.

3 tbsp (45 ml) olive oil

½ yellow onion, roughly chopped

2 cloves garlic, chopped

4 large carrots, peeled and chopped into 1-inch (2.5-cm) pieces

½ tsp cumin

½ tsp coriander

½ tsp turmeric

¼ tsp ground cinnamon

¾ tsp kosher salt

½ tsp ground black pepper

4 cups (960 ml) low-sodium vegetable stock

FOR SERVING

Full-fat plain yogurt

Pomegranate molasses

Olive oil

Chopped fresh cilantro leaves

Heat a tall Dutch oven over medium heat, and add the olive oil. Add the onion, and sauté for 4 to 5 minutes, until softened. Add the garlic, and sauté for another minute. Add the carrots, cumin, coriander, turmeric, cinnamon, salt and pepper, and give everything a good stir.

Pour in the vegetable stock, making sure all of the vegetables are completely submerged. Cover the Dutch oven with a lid, leaving a small opening.

Bring the soup to a boil, then reduce the heat to a simmer, and cook until the carrots are incredibly tender and can easily be pierced with a fork, 30 to 40 minutes. Once the carrots are cooked, turn off the heat, and blend the soup with an immersion blender. You can also ladle the soup into a blender and pour it back into the Dutch oven.

Once the carrot soup is smooth, ladle the soup into bowls, and garnish with a drizzle of yogurt, pomegranate molasses, olive oil and sprinkle of cilantro.

GREEN SHAKSHUKA WITH ZA'ATAR AND FETA

YIELDS
2 to 4
servings

I am always looking for ways to use an abundance of garden greens. Of course, stuffing them inside a Savory Dutch Oven Spinach Pie (page 115) is usually my first thought, but a hearty vegetable-filled shakshuka is next on the list.

Sautéed greens are wilted down, allowing for the eggs to gently poach on top. I also like whisking olive oil with za'atar and drizzling it on top, another reason to sop up the delicious flavors with bread.

3 tbsp (45 ml) olive oil

1 leek, white and light green parts only, thinly sliced

2 cloves garlic, finely chopped

1 zucchini, grated and squeezed of excess moisture

4 cups (120 g) baby spinach and/or kale

¾ tsp kosher salt

½ tsp ground black pepper

½ tsp za'atar

¼ tsp cumin

5 eggs

½ cup (75 g) crumbled feta

FOR SERVING

Za'atar

Aleppo pepper

Chopped fresh parsley leaves

Olive oil

Toasted bread

Heat a Dutch oven over medium heat, and add the olive oil. Add the leek, and sauté until very soft, 6 to 8 minutes. Add the garlic, and sauté for another minute, until fragrant. Add the grated zucchini and continue sautéing for 1 to 2 minutes until softened. Add the spinach, in batches, and sauté until the greens are just wilted. Season with salt, pepper, za'atar and cumin, and give everything a good stir.

Make five wells in the vegetables with the back of a spoon, and gently crack an egg into each well.

Cover the Dutch oven, leaving a small opening, which will assist in cooking the tops of the eggs. Continue cooking until the eggs are just set, 5 to 7 minutes, or until desired doneness.

Once done, turn off the heat, and top the shakshuka with the crumbled feta while still warm. To serve, garnish the shakshuka with a sprinkle of za'atar, Aleppo pepper, chopped parsley and a drizzle of olive oil. Serve with toasted bread on the side to sop up the delicious green shakshuka.

 TIP: Depending on the size of your Dutch oven, you can adjust the number of eggs. A wider Dutch oven or braiser will fit up to 8 eggs.

SMOKY MOROCCAN EGGPLANT AND TOMATO DIP (ZAALOUK)

YIELDS
2 to 4
servings

Get the pita ready because you won't be able to resist slathering this creamy, smoky eggplant dip all over toasted bread. Don't skip the lemon, as it makes the deep flavors of the eggplant and spices pop with brightness.

This would be a fantastic mezze to serve alongside Garlic-Lemon Chicken with Saffron Pearl Couscous and Zucchini (page 26) or Cinnamon-Spiced Rice with Lamb and Almonds (page 53).

3 tbsp (45 ml) olive oil

2 cloves garlic, finely chopped

2 tbsp (32 g) tomato paste

1 tsp coriander

1 tsp smoked paprika

½ tsp cumin

½ tsp Aleppo pepper

¾ tsp kosher salt

2 medium vine tomatoes, chopped into small cubes

1 medium eggplant, peeled and cut into small cubes

½ lemon, zested and juiced

Small bunch fresh parsley, leaves roughly chopped

½ cup (120 ml) water

FOR SERVING

Olive oil

Fresh cilantro leaves

Aleppo pepper

Lemon zest

Sumac

Oil-cured olives

Warm pita bread

Heat a tall Dutch oven over medium heat, and add the olive oil. Add the garlic, and sauté for 1 to 2 minutes, until lightly caramelized. Stir in the tomato paste, and sauté for another minute, then stir in the coriander, smoked paprika, cumin, Aleppo pepper and salt. Continue sautéing for another 30 seconds. Add the tomatoes, eggplant, lemon zest, lemon juice and parsley, and stir together so everything is coated with the spiced oil. Pour in the water, and give everything one final stir.

Place a lid on the Dutch oven, leaving a small opening, and bring to a simmer. Continue cooking the vegetables for 20 minutes, until the eggplant and tomatoes are incredibly soft.

Once done, turn the heat off, and use a potato masher or the back of a spatula to mash the eggplant and tomatoes, creating a thick dip. Ladle the zaalouk into shallow bowls, and garnish with a drizzle of olive oil and some cilantro, Aleppo pepper, lemon zest and sumac. Place briny oil-cured olives on the side, or garnish the eggplant dip with a few of the olives. Serve the zaalouk warm or at room temperature with warm pita bread.

ZA'ATAR-ROASTED BEETS AND SWEET POTATOES OVER LABNEH

YIELDS
2 to 4
servings

"When in doubt, roast it," is what I like to say when I have a pile of root vegetables that need to be used. Roasting brings out the natural sugars, and the outside caramelizes while keeping the middle tender and, honestly, quite addictive.

Labneh cheese is a strained yogurt cheese that is tangier and thicker than Greek yogurt. I highly recommend looking for labneh, as it is becoming more accessible in Western stores.

2 medium red beets, peeled and cut into ½-inch (1.3-cm) pieces

1 medium sweet potato, peeled and cut into ½-inch (1.3-cm) cubes

2 tbsp (20 g) za'atar, plus more for garnish

1 tsp cumin

1 tsp kosher salt

½ tsp ground black pepper

¼ cup (60 ml) olive oil

Labneh cheese, for serving

Fresh mint leaves, for garnish

Preheat the oven to 400°F (204°C), and line a baking sheet with parchment paper or aluminum foil. Scatter the beets and sweet potato on the baking sheet, and season with za'atar, cumin, salt and pepper. Drizzle with olive oil. Give the vegetables a good toss, making sure the spices are evenly coated, and spread the vegetables into a single layer.

Roast the vegetables for 40 to 45 minutes, until the beets and sweet potato are fork-tender and lightly caramelized.

To serve, spread a generous layer of labneh cheese onto a serving platter, and top with the roasted vegetables. Sprinkle with additional za'atar, and garnish with fresh mint leaves.

SMOKY VEGETABLE BEAN STEW WITH BROILED HALLOUMI

YIELDS
4 to 6
servings

Smoked paprika, tender vegetables and creamy beans make for a great, hearty vegetarian meal. The halloumi topping is key, and because halloumi holds up to high-heat cooking, it can handle a good run under the broiler to achieve a nice crispy, cheesy topping. And may I suggest grabbing a good hunk of crusty bread to sop up the delicious smoky sauce?

3 tbsp (45 ml) olive oil

½ white onion, diced

2 cloves garlic, finely chopped

1 red bell pepper, seeds removed, cut into ½-inch (1.3-cm) cubes

2 medium zucchini, cut into ½-inch (1.3-cm) cubes

½ tsp dried thyme

½ tsp smoked paprika

1 (15.5-oz [439-g]) can chopped tomatoes

1 (15.5-oz [439-g]) can Great Northern or white beans, drained and rinsed

2 cups (480 ml) low-sodium vegetable stock

¾ tsp kosher salt

8 oz (226 g) halloumi cheese, cut into ½-inch (1.3-cm) cubes

FOR SERVING
Chopped fresh parsley leaves

Toasted bread

Preheat the oven to 400°F (204°C). Heat a Dutch oven over medium heat, and add the olive oil. Add the onion, and sauté for 3 to 4 minutes, until softened. Add the garlic, and sauté for 1 to 2 minutes, until fragrant. Add the bell pepper and zucchini, and season the vegetables with thyme and smoked paprika. Sauté the vegetables for 8 to 10 minutes, until just tender.

Pour in the tomatoes, beans and vegetable stock, and season with salt. Give everything a good stir, and continue simmering for 10 to 15 minutes, until the sauce thickens slightly.

Scatter the cubes of halloumi cheese on top of the vegetable stew, and place in the oven for 10 minutes, or until the halloumi is lightly golden brown. You can also place it under the broiler for 3 to 4 minutes, until the cheese just melts.

Once done, garnish the vegetable stew with chopped parsley, and serve warm along with toasted bread.

ROASTED CAULIFLOWER AND CABBAGE WITH PRESERVED LEMON

YIELDS
4
servings

This flavorful vegetable side dish can take on any main course. Cauliflower and cabbage are seasoned with the bold flavors of sumac and turmeric and roasted until just crisp and tender. But the taste bud explosions come from the salty preserved lemon and sweet pomegranate seeds.

There are all sorts of variations you can do, such as adding toasted pine nuts or dried currants or even a final drizzle of pomegranate molasses for a sweet and tart finish. This recipe can also be served warm or at room temperature, making it an easy addition to dinner parties.

1 medium head cauliflower, cut into ½-inch (1.3-cm) florets

½ red cabbage, cut into ½-inch (1.3-cm) wedges

¼ cup (60 ml) olive oil

1 tsp kosher salt

¾ tsp sumac

¾ tsp turmeric

½ tsp garlic powder

½ tsp ground black pepper

¼ cup (60 g) chopped preserved lemon, seeds removed

Small bunch fresh parsley or cilantro, leaves roughly chopped

FOR SERVING

Olive oil

Aleppo pepper

Pomegranate seeds

Preheat the oven to 400°F (204°C) and line a baking sheet with parchment paper or aluminum foil. Add the cauliflower and cabbage to the baking sheet, drizzle with the olive oil and season with the salt, sumac, turmeric, garlic powder and black pepper. Give everything a good toss so the spices evenly coat the vegetables. Roast for 40 minutes, until the cauliflower is tender and the cabbage is slightly caramelized.

Once done, remove from the oven, and transfer the roasted cauliflower and cabbage to a wide bowl or platter, along with the preserved lemon and parsley. Stir to combine.

Garnish the roasted vegetables with another generous drizzle of olive oil, Aleppo pepper and pomegranate seeds.

 TIP: If preserved lemons aren't available, add the zest of half a lemon, or more to taste.

SAVORY DUTCH OVEN SPINACH PIE

YIELDS
6 to 8
servings

Bourekas or *boreks* are popular savory pasties in Turkey. Similar to the Greek spanakopita, many boreks are filled with spinach and feta cheese. But what makes boreks slightly different and, personally, more satisfying is the addition of melty mozzarella cheese and a milky-rich glaze that coats the phyllo layers, providing a more tender bite.

2 lb (907 g) frozen spinach, thawed and squeezed of excess moisture

⅓ cup (17 g) fresh dill, roughly chopped

⅓ cup (20 g) fresh parsley, leaves roughly chopped

⅓ cup (30 g) fresh mint, roughly chopped

½ lb (226 g) low-moisture mozzarella cheese, shredded

¾ cup (113 g) crumbled feta

1 packet phyllo dough, thawed

Nigella seeds or sesame seeds, for garnish

GLAZE
½ cup (113 g) unsalted butter, melted and cooled

½ cup (120 ml) whole milk

2 eggs

2 tbsp (30 ml) olive oil

Preheat the oven to 350°F (176°C).

In a large bowl, add the spinach, dill, parsley, mint, mozzarella and feta, and give everything a good mix so all of the cheese is evenly distributed.

In another bowl or measuring cup, make the glaze. Add the melted butter, milk, eggs and olive oil, and whisk to combine.

Unfold the thawed phyllo, keeping a damp towel over the sheets so they don't dry out as you layer. Brush a thin layer of the glaze on the bottom of a wide Dutch oven, and lay two phyllo sheets on the bottom of the Dutch oven, folding in the corners. Brush another layer of the glaze on the phyllo sheets, and continue alternating the phyllo and glaze until you are a little over halfway through the phyllo sheets.

Add all of the spinach and cheese filling on top of the stacked phyllo sheets, and spread the spinach mixture out into an even layer. Continue layering and alternating the phyllo sheets with the glaze, reserving some of the glaze for the final top layer.

Use a sharp knife to carefully cut the spinach pie into 15 to 18 squares or triangles. The phyllo is delicate, so take your time. Garnish each square with a small sprinkle of nigella seeds or sesame seeds. Bake the spinach pie, uncovered, for 45 to 50 minutes, until the phyllo is lightly golden brown and crisp.

Once done, remove the spinach pie from the oven, and cool for at least 10 minutes before serving. Enjoy the spinach pie either warm or at room temperature.

 TIP: Don't be intimidated by working with phyllo sheets. Keep a damp towel over the sheets as you work with them, and if one breaks or cracks, that's OK. No one will know once it's baked.

CHAPTER 5

GRAINS, BEANS AND SOME PASTA, TOO

Staples in Mediterranean cooking, grains, beans and pasta are always stocked in our pantry. Couscous cooks up in the amount of time that water is hot and welcomes additions such as vegetables and golden raisins (page 131).

Basmati rice is found throughout the book and is the preferred style thanks to its aromatic flavor, long grains and airy texture. If you have an abundance of basmati rice, try the One-Pot Mujadara with Crispy Leeks (Lebanese Rice and Lentils; page 124). Lentils and rice simmer together, and the crispy leeks transform the humble dish into something filling and flavorful.

Hearty Tuscan Kale Soup with Farro (page 136) is loaded with beans and nutty farro. This is a perfect soup to make a large batch of and freeze for when you need a quick dinner on the table.

If you love comforting pasta dishes, the Whipped Feta Pasta with Sweet Cherry Tomatoes (page 139) is the perfect comforting meal. Burst cherry tomatoes are paired with a tangy labneh cheese sauce, giving you all those "mac and cheese" feels without the heaviness.

And for an impressive and easy side dish, try the Zucchini and Herb Pilaf (page 135) that is loaded with fresh herbs and functions as a great side dish to pair with other main dishes.

BAKED RISOTTO WITH SPINACH AND FETA

YIELDS
4
servings

There is nothing more comforting than a well-made risotto. Traditionally, risotto is made on the stovetop, and the trick is to consistently stir the starchy rice as you ladle in hot broth, thus creating a creamy product. Once the aromatics, rice and broth are stirred in, the oven does all the work.

And don't skip on adding the final garnishes. A few sprigs of fresh dill and a squeeze of fresh lemon juice wake up the comforting flavors with a pop of brightness.

2 tbsp (30 ml) olive oil

1 large leek, white and light green parts only, thinly sliced

2 cloves garlic, finely chopped

1 cup (200 g) arborio rice

1 tsp lemon zest

1 tbsp (15 ml) lemon juice, plus more for serving

¾ tsp kosher salt

½ tsp ground black pepper

5 cups (1.2 L) vegetable stock

4 cups (120 g) fresh baby spinach

½ cup (75 g) feta cheese, roughly crumbled

¼ cup (15 g) fresh dill, roughly chopped, plus more for garnish

Preheat the oven to 375°F (190°C), and heat a Dutch oven over medium-high heat.

Add the olive oil and leek, and sauté for 5 to 8 minutes, until softened. Add the garlic, and sauté for another minute. Stir in the arborio rice, and sauté for 1 minute so all of the rice grains are coated with the oil. Add the lemon zest, lemon juice, salt, pepper and vegetable stock. Give everything one good stir, and cover with the lid.

Bake the risotto for 35 minutes, until the rice is cooked through and creamy. Remove the pot from the oven, and stir in the spinach. The heat from the rice will slowly wilt the spinach.

Add the feta cheese and fresh dill, and stir to combine. Garnish with a squeeze of fresh lemon juice and additional fresh dill.

CREAMY MASCARPONE POLENTA

YIELDS
4
servings

This is the recipe to make when you need something comforting, quick and delicious. Polenta cooks up in the time it takes to boil water, and you can customize it to your liking. Here, I add thick mascarpone cheese and Parmesan to give creaminess and savoriness to the simple polenta. You can also stir in labneh cheese or a drizzle of heavy cream.

Serve alongside Turmeric-Braised Short Ribs with Red Wine and Dates (page 41) or Braciole Stuffed with Pine Nuts and Parmesan (page 58).

4 cups (960 ml) low-sodium vegetable stock

1 cup (125 g) polenta

¼ cup (58 g) mascarpone cheese

¼ cup (25 g) grated Parmesan

½ tsp kosher salt

¼ tsp ground black pepper

Olive oil, for garnish

Fresh chives, finely chopped, for garnish

In a tall Dutch oven, add the vegetable stock, and bring it up to a boil. Once boiling, whisk in the polenta and reduce the heat to maintain a simmer. Continue whisking the polenta until thickened, 3 to 5 minutes.

Turn the heat off, and stir in the mascarpone cheese, Parmesan cheese, salt and pepper. Continue mixing until the cheese is well combined and the polenta is creamy.

Ladle the creamy polenta into wide bowls, and garnish with a drizzle of olive oil and a sprinkle of chopped chives.

 TIP: When buying polenta, you'll see both polenta and cornmeal at the store, and either can be used. If you prefer an even creamier and finer texture, take the extra step and grind the polenta in a food processor or blender.

SUMMERY PUTTANESCA PASTA WITH BURST CHERRY TOMATOES

YIELDS
4
servings

Salty, savory and briny are some of my favorite flavors. Typically, puttanesca is made with a thicker marinara with specks of olives and capers. This lighter, more summery version showcases all of those same full flavors with a slightly sweeter note, thanks to the burst cherry tomatoes.

If you are nervous about adding the anchovies, don't be. When anchovies are simmered with garlic and oil, the noticeable pungent flavor melts away, and what's left is a subtle umami that blends well with the other brinier ingredients in the dish.

3 tbsp (45 ml) olive oil

1 small shallot, diced

3 anchovy fillets

1 large clove garlic, finely chopped

1 pint (298 g) cherry tomatoes, halved

¼ cup (30 g) capers, plus more for garnish

¾ cup (135 g) pitted Castelvetrano olives, roughly chopped

12 oz (340 g) spaghetti or linguine

5 cups (1.2 L) low-sodium vegetable stock

½ cup (50 g) grated Parmesan cheese

Fresh basil leaves, for garnish

Heat a wide Dutch oven over medium heat, and add the olive oil.

Once the oil is hot, add the shallot, and sauté until softened, about 3 minutes.

Add the anchovy fillets and garlic, and sauté until the anchovies have broken down and melted into the sauce, another minute.

Add the cherry tomatoes, capers, olives, spaghetti and vegetable stock. Use tongs to gently push down on the pasta, making sure all of the noodles are submerged in the liquid.

Bring to a boil, and stir the pasta every few minutes until the liquid has absorbed, about 10 minutes. Once the pasta is cooked, stir in the Parmesan, and garnish with additional capers and fresh basil.

 TIP: Notice there is no salt added in the recipe. The capers, olives and anchovies all provide enough salt, though taste for seasoning and add a pinch if you like.

ONE-POT MUJADARA WITH CRISPY LEEKS (LEBANESE RICE AND LENTILS)

YIELDS
4
servings

Mujadara is a simple Lebanese dish with rice, lentils and crispy onions. Usually, mujadara is made using multiple pots: one for the rice, another for the lentils and yet another for browning the onions. I've simplified it to one pot, and my version has a slight twist: using crispy leeks instead of the traditional onions. I highly suggest making an extra batch of the crispy leeks, as you won't want to stop snacking on them. The dish is fantastic served alongside Dutch Oven Roast Chicken with Preserved Lemon Compound Butter (page 21) or Turmeric-Braised Short Ribs with Red Wine and Dates (page 41).

2 tbsp (30 ml) olive oil

1 large leek, white and light green parts only, thinly sliced

4½ cups (1.1 L) low-sodium vegetable stock

¾ cup (144 g) dry brown lentils

1 cup (200 g) uncooked basmati rice

½ tsp turmeric

½ tsp cumin

¾ tsp kosher salt

Chopped fresh parsley leaves, for garnish

In a tall Dutch oven over medium heat, add the olive oil. Once the oil is shimmering, add the leek, and sauté until golden brown and crispy, 6 to 8 minutes. Transfer to a plate and set aside.

Pour the vegetable stock in, and bring to a boil. Add the lentils, and cover with a lid, leaving a small opening. Reduce the heat to a simmer, and cook for 10 to 15 minutes, until the lentils are halfway cooked. Stir in the basmati rice, turmeric, cumin and salt. Place a few sheets of paper towels under the lid, which will help soak up any additional moisture, creating a fluffier rice.

Continue cooking for another 15 minutes, until the rice and lentils are cooked through and tender. Once done, remove from the heat, and fluff the rice and lentils with a fork. Stir in the crispy leeks, and garnish with parsley.

TIP: Spring and summer leeks are tender and flavorful, and that is the time when I buy them in bulk and prep for later use. Once cleaned and sliced, leeks hold up very well in the freezer and can be added to sautés easily without thawing.

JEWELED BULGUR SALAD WITH CITRUS VINAIGRETTE

YIELDS
4
servings

If you are looking for an easy grain to add to salads or just about anything, try bulgur. Usually added to tabbouleh, bulgur cooks up incredibly quickly and takes on any flavors you give it. Bulgur holds up very well, and I would even suggest making a large batch and adding it to various salads throughout the week.

2 cups (480 ml) low-sodium vegetable stock or water

1 cup (140 g) dried bulgur

1 medium tomato, diced

1 medium roasted beet, peeled and diced

1 Persian cucumber, diced

½ cup (87 g) pomegranate seeds

½ cup (50 g) pistachios, roughly chopped

LEMON VINAIGRETTE

½ cup (120 ml) olive oil

Zest and juice of 1 lemon

1 tsp honey

½ tsp kosher salt

⅛ tsp ground black pepper

FOR SERVING

Lemon wedges

Fresh mint leaves

In a tall Dutch oven, add the vegetable stock, and bring it to a boil. Once boiling, turn off the heat, and stir in the bulgur. Cover the Dutch oven with a lid, and let the bulgur finish cooking for 15 minutes, or until all the liquid has absorbed.

While the bulgur is cooking, make the vinaigrette. In a medium bowl, whisk the olive oil, lemon zest, lemon juice, honey, salt and pepper until emulsified and well combined. You can also use a mason jar to shake up the vinaigrette.

Fluff the bulgur with a fork, and add the tomato, beet, cucumber, pomegranate seeds and pistachios. Pour the lemon vinaigrette over everything, and toss to combine. Taste for seasoning, and adjust as needed. Transfer the bulgur salad to a platter, and serve with lemon wedges and fresh mint.

TIPS: Store-bought roasted beets make this recipe a breeze. If you prefer to roast your own beets, trim and wash the beets well, and wrap them tightly in foil. Roast the beets at 400°F (204°C) until they can easily be pierced with a knife, 45 to 55 minutes. Then let the beets cool, peel them and chop them into cubes.

Persian cucumbers are used in this recipe because they are far less watery than traditional cucumbers and also have a more delicate peel. If Persian cucumbers are not available, look for long English cucumbers that have a similar structure. And if the more common slicing cucumbers are only available, I suggest peeling and scooping out the seeds.

WARM QUINOA SALAD WITH FRIED HALLOUMI AND FIGS

YIELDS
2 large salads

Halloumi is a firm sheep's milk cheese from Cyprus that holds up well to high heat cooking and doesn't melt, making it great for pan-frying, grilling or adding on top of vegetable and bean bakes (page 111).

You can often find halloumi in specialty grocery stores, and it's becoming even more well-known and easily found in traditional stores, too. When you buy halloumi, it will have some brine in the package, so be sure to drain that and dry the cheese very well before cooking so it develops a gorgeous deep and caramelized crust.

1 tbsp (15 ml) olive oil or avocado oil

1 block halloumi, cut into thick slices

2 cups (480 ml) low-sodium vegetable stock or water

1 cup (170 g) quinoa

2 cups (40 g) baby arugula

6 to 8 figs, halved or quartered

½ cup (50 g) chopped pistachios

½ cup (65 g) dried cranberries or currants

HONEY-BALSAMIC VINAIGRETTE

½ cup (120 ml) olive oil

2 tbsp (30 ml) balsamic vinegar

1 tsp honey

½ tsp kosher salt

Ground black pepper

Heat a Dutch oven over medium heat, and add the oil. While the oil is heating up, pat the halloumi dry with paper towels. Once the oil is hot, add the halloumi slices, and fry until a deep golden crust forms on both sides, 2 to 3 minutes per side. Transfer the halloumi to a cutting board. Once the halloumi is cool enough to handle, cut it into cubes.

In the same Dutch oven, add the vegetable stock, and bring it to a boil. Add the quinoa, and reduce the heat to a simmer. Cook the quinoa until tender and the liquid has absorbed, 15 to 20 minutes.

While the quinoa is cooking, make the balsamic vinaigrette. In a small bowl, whisk the olive oil, balsamic vinegar, honey, salt and pepper until well combined. You can also add the vinaigrette ingredients to a mason jar and shake until combined.

Once the quinoa is finished cooking, remove it from the heat, and add the arugula. Pour the vinaigrette over the salad while the quinoa is still warm, and fluff with a fork to combine. Transfer the quinoa to a platter or wide bowl along with the figs, pistachios, dried cranberries and halloumi cheese, and serve.

VEGETABLE COUSCOUS WITH ZA'ATAR AND GOLDEN RAISINS

YIELDS
4 to 6
servings

If you are looking for an aromatic, flavorful and stunning vegetarian dish, this one has got you covered. Colorful vegetables are sautéed with earthy turmeric and za'atar. Sweet peas and golden raisins plump up and offer a bite of something sweet every so often, leaving an explosion of textures and bold flavors.

This would be an impressive side dish to pair with pomegranate lamb shanks (page 46) or alongside Dutch Oven Roast Chicken with Preserved Lemon Compound Butter (page 21).

3 tbsp (45 ml) olive oil

½ small red onion, finely diced

2 to 3 cloves garlic, finely chopped

2 medium carrots, peeled and cut into small cubes

1 red or orange bell pepper, seeded and diced

1 medium yellow squash or zucchini, cut into small cubes

¾ tsp kosher salt

½ tsp ground black pepper

1 tsp za'atar

½ tsp turmeric

1½ cups (360 ml) low-sodium vegetable stock

1½ cups (260 g) couscous

½ cup (67 g) frozen and thawed peas

½ cup (54 g) toasted slivered almonds

½ cup (73 g) golden raisins

¼ cup (15 g) fresh parsley leaves, chopped

¼ cup (25 g) fresh mint leaves, chopped

Heat a medium Dutch oven over medium-high heat, and add the olive oil. Add the onion, and sauté for 3 to 4 minutes to soften. Add the garlic, and sauté for another minute. Stir in the carrots, bell pepper and squash, and season with salt and pepper. Give everything a good mix, and continue cooking for 4 to 5 minutes so the squash and carrots begin to soften. Stir in the za'atar and turmeric, and give everything a good stir, making sure the spices evenly coat all of the vegetables.

Increase the heat to high, pour in the vegetable stock and bring it to a boil. As soon as the stock is boiling, turn off the heat, and immediately pour in the couscous. Use a spoon to evenly distribute the couscous, and top with the peas, almonds and golden raisins. Cover with a lid, and allow the couscous to absorb the stock for 8 to 10 minutes.

Once all the liquid has absorbed, the couscous should be puffed up and tender. Fluff the couscous with a fork, being careful not to disrupt the vegetables too much. Stir in the chopped parsley and mint to serve.

CUMIN-SCENTED LENTIL SOUP

YIELDS
4 to 6
servings

I have fond memories of ordering Greek lentil soup when I was younger and marveling at all the flavors, the warm spices and the creamy texture of the lentils. It was the most comforting soup and still is. Now that I am older and have a more experienced palate, I took to those memories when creating the flavors of this memorable lentil soup. The warm cumin and earthy paprika transform the humble lentils into something satisfying and soothing, and I hope you enjoy this soup as much as I do reliving it.

3 tbsp (45 ml) olive oil

½ yellow onion, diced

1 large celery stalk, diced

2 medium carrots, peeled and chopped into ½-inch (1.3-cm) pieces

2 cloves garlic, finely chopped

2 tbsp (32 g) tomato paste

1 tsp paprika

1 tsp cumin

½ tsp dried oregano

1 bay leaf

1½ cups (285 g) brown lentils

5 cups (1.2 L) low-sodium vegetable stock

1 tsp kosher salt

½ tsp ground black pepper

A few dashes of red wine vinegar or lemon juice

Chopped fresh parsley leaves, for garnish

Heat a Dutch oven over medium heat, and add the olive oil. Add the onion and celery, and sauté until softened but not caramelized, 3 to 4 minutes. Add the carrots, and continue sautéing for another 2 to 3 minutes. Stir in the garlic, and sauté for another minute, until the garlic is fragrant but not too browned.

Add the tomato paste, paprika, cumin and oregano, and give everything a good stir, breaking down the tomato paste and spices into the oil. Add the bay leaf and lentils, pour in the vegetable stock and season with salt and pepper.

Cover the Dutch oven with a lid, leaving a small opening, and bring the soup to a boil. Then reduce the heat to a simmer, and cook for 40 to 45 minutes, until the lentils are tender and the vegetables are just cooked through.

Once the soup is done, remove the bay leaf, and add a few dashes of red wine vinegar or lemon juice. Ladle the lentil soup into bowls, and garnish with parsley.

TIP: Don't skimp on the final splash of vinegar right at the end. The bright acidity wakes up the heavier lentils. If you don't have vinegar, add a splash of lemon juice, but a little goes a long way.

ZUCCHINI AND HERB PILAF

YIELDS
4
servings

This is an easy and impressive side dish that goes with just about anything. I often make this with Dutch Oven Roast Chicken with Preserved Lemon Compound Butter (page 21) when I want something delicious but unfussy. You can also use other quick-cooking vegetables instead of the zucchini, such as tender baby spinach, summer squash or even a few handfuls of sweet peas.

2 tbsp (30 g) ghee or unsalted butter

2 tbsp (30 ml) olive oil

1 small shallot, diced

½ cup (54 g) slivered almonds

2 cloves garlic, finely chopped

¾ cup (150 g) uncooked basmati rice

¼ cup (28 g) orzo

1 medium zucchini, cut into ½-inch (1.3-cm) pieces

Zest and juice of 1 lemon

1 tsp kosher salt

½ tsp ground black pepper

2 cups (480 ml) low-sodium vegetable stock

Small bunch fresh parsley or mint, leaves roughly chopped

Heat a tall Dutch oven over medium heat, and add the ghee and olive oil. Once the ghee melts, add the shallot, and sauté for 2 to 3 minutes, until the shallot begins to soften. Add the slivered almonds, and sauté for another 2 minutes, tossing the nuts around the oil and ghee so they begin to toast. Add the garlic, and cook for another minute.

Stir in the basmati rice and orzo, and sauté everything for another 1 to 2 minutes, making sure all of the grains and nuts are coated with the flavorful oil. Add the zucchini, lemon zest, lemon juice, salt and pepper, and give everything another stir.

Pour in the vegetable stock, and give everything a good stir once more. Bring the mixture to a boil, then reduce the heat to a simmer. Cover the Dutch oven, leaving a small opening, and cook the pilaf for 15 minutes, or until all of the liquid is absorbed and the rice and orzo are cooked through and tender.

Once done, turn off heat, and stir in the chopped herbs to serve.

HEARTY TUSCAN KALE SOUP WITH FARRO

YIELDS
4
servings

Typically, Tuscan soup has chunks of sausage and a creamy base. My version is a lighter take but is still substantial and delicious. Farro is a great addition to soups, as it plumps up and becomes chewy and tender. Shredded kale can handle the longer simmer and still hold up with the other hardier elements of the soup. And if you can find fire-roasted tomatoes, use those. The additional flavor of the charred tomatoes works well with the smoked paprika.

3 tbsp (45 ml) olive oil

½ red onion, diced

½ fennel bulb, diced

2 medium carrots, peeled and chopped into ½-inch (1.3-cm) cubes

3 cloves garlic, finely chopped or grated

¾ tsp kosher salt

½ tsp ground black pepper

1 tsp dried thyme

½ tsp dried oregano

½ tsp smoked paprika

1 small bunch kale, leaves removed and shredded

½ cup (75 g) uncooked farro

1 (15.5-oz [439-g]) can white beans, drained and rinsed

1 (15.5-oz [439-g]) can chopped fire-roasted tomatoes

4½ cups (1.1 L) low-sodium vegetable stock

Small Parmesan rind

1 bay leaf

Grated Parmesan, for serving

Heat a tall Dutch oven over medium heat, and add the olive oil. Add the onion, and sauté for 2 to 3 minutes, until softened but not caramelized. Add the fennel and carrots, and continue sautéing for another 3 to 4 minutes, until the vegetables become fragrant.

Stir in the garlic, salt, pepper, thyme, oregano and smoked paprika, and continue sautéing for another minute, waking up the dried herbs. Add the kale, and sauté for another minute, until the leaves wilt. Add the farro and white beans, and give everything another stir so all of the farro and beans are coated with the infused oil.

Pour in the fire-roasted tomatoes and vegetable stock, and nestle in the Parmesan rind and bay leaf. Cover the Dutch oven with the lid, leaving a small opening. Bring the soup to a boil, then reduce the heat to a constant simmer, and continue cooking the soup for 55 minutes to 1 hour, until the farro is cooked through and the vegetables are tender.

Once done, remove the bay leaf and Parmesan rind, and ladle the soup into bowls. Garnish with grated Parmesan, and serve.

TIP: Parmesan rinds are a fantastic addition to soups, stews and sauces. As soon as you're done grating a chunk of Parmesan, save the tougher rind to add to soups and sauces. As the soup simmers, flecks of Parmesan dissolve in the soup, giving another layer of savory, cheesy flavor.

WHIPPED FETA PASTA WITH SWEET CHERRY TOMATOES

YIELDS
4
servings

This is one of those dishes that just hits when you are craving something creamy and comforting. Tangy labneh is the star of this easy, creamy feta sauce, and if you can find a tub of labneh cheese, grab some and always keep it on hand. Truth be told, I could eat labneh cheese by the spoonful or serve it simply with Za'atar-Roasted Beets and Sweet Potatoes over Labneh (page 108) or as a dip with za'atar and olive oil. If you don't have labneh cheese, whole-milk plain Greek yogurt also makes for an ultra-creamy pasta sauce.

1 tsp kosher salt

8 oz (226 g) short-shaped pasta, such as fusilli or orecchiette

3 tbsp (45 ml) olive oil, divided

2 cloves garlic, finely chopped

1 pint (298 g) cherry tomatoes, large ones cut in half

WHIPPED FETA

1 cup (150 g) crumbled feta

¾ cup (168 g) labneh or Greek yogurt

1 tsp lemon juice

½ tsp kosher salt

½ tsp ground black pepper

FOR SERVING

Fresh basil leaves

Aleppo pepper

Olive oil

Bring a large pot of water to a boil, and add the salt. Once boiling, add the pasta, and cook for 1 to 2 minutes less than the package directions.

When the pasta is done cooking, reserve 1 cup (240 ml) of the starchy cooking water, and drain the pasta. Drizzle the cooked pasta with 1 tablespoon (15 ml) of the olive oil, and give it a toss so the pasta doesn't stick together.

Meanwhile, make the whipped feta sauce. In a food processor or blender, combine the feta, labneh, lemon juice, salt and pepper, and blend until smooth.

Place the same pot over medium heat, and add the remaining 2 tablespoons (30 ml) of olive oil. Add the garlic, and sauté for 1 to 2 minutes, until fragrant but not caramelized. Add the cherry tomatoes, stirring them into the garlic oil, and continue cooking, until the tomatoes plump up and some begin to burst. Add the cooked pasta to the garlic and tomatoes, and give everything a toss so the tomatoes are coated with the garlic oil.

Pour in the whipped feta sauce, and give everything a good toss. Stir in a few tablespoons (45 ml) of starchy pasta water, and add more to reach a creamy consistency, up to ½ cup (120 ml).

Ladle the pasta into bowls, and garnish with basil leaves, Aleppo pepper and an extra drizzle of olive oil.

 TIP: Look for feta that is packed in brine, which is creamier than the pre-crumbled options.

CHAPTER 6

FRESH AND CRISP SALADS ON THE SIDE

Almost every recipe in this book is a complete meal, but sometimes you want a bright, fresh and crisp salad to complement a dish.

Turkish Shepherd's Salad with Fresh Herbs and Sumac (page 160) is bright, lemony and crisp and the perfect addition to Cardamom Chicken Thighs with Basmati Rice and Pine Nuts (page 18).

The Mediterranean Chopped Salad with Creamy Tahini (page 144) is a play on a chopped salad and tahini sauce, combining the two together. Besides wanting to eat this all on its own with warm pita bread (I may have done that quite a few times), this salad can be served alongside just about anything, but I strongly recommend serving it with the Lemony Za'atar Chicken and Potatoes (page 29) for a truly incredible flavor pairing.

And if you are looking for a true flavor explosion, try the Chunky Beet Salad with Walnuts and Cilantro Vinaigrette (page 163), which is a simple take on a popular Turkish mezze. You can either roast your own beets or utilize store-bought cooked beets to make this salad even easier.

CUCUMBER YOGURT SALAD WITH MINT AND PISTACHIOS

YIELDS
2 to 4
servings

I grew up eating a cucumber yogurt dip similar to Greek tzatziki. My mom and I have made it all sorts of ways over the years: sometimes with grated cucumber or small chunks, sometimes with fresh mint or dried dill, but always with a good splash of fresh lemon juice.

In my version, cucumbers are thinly sliced, keeping them crunchy and intact. The creamy cucumber salad is topped with mint and dill and a handful of chopped pistachios, which give the salad a delicious nuttiness.

Serve the cucumber yogurt salad alongside Greek Chicken with Rice and Olives (page 13) or with Moroccan Meatballs with Saffron Couscous (page 54).

½ cup (120 ml) Greek yogurt

2 tbsp (30 ml) lemon juice

½ tsp kosher salt

¼ cup (25 g) chopped fresh mint, plus more for garnish

¼ cup (15 g) chopped fresh dill, plus more garnish

1 English cucumber, thinly sliced

½ medium red onion, thinly sliced

2 tbsp (14 g) chopped pistachios, for garnish

2 tbsp (30 ml) olive oil, for garnish

In a medium bowl, add the yogurt, lemon juice, salt, mint and dill, and whisk to combine. Fold in the cucumber and red onion so all the vegetables are evenly coated.

Serve the cucumber salad in a wide bowl, and garnish with pistachios, mint, dill and a final drizzle of olive oil.

MEDITERRANEAN CHOPPED SALAD WITH CREAMY TAHINI

YIELDS
4
servings

This crunchy and lemony chopped salad is served right in the center of a creamy tahini sauce. This is a perfect accompaniment to Stuffed Grape Leaves with Ground Beef, Herbs and Dried Fruit (page 57) or Cinnamon-Spiced Rice with Lamb and Almonds (page 53), but also I've been known to just enjoy this on its own. Creamy, fresh, crunchy and garlicky, is there anything better?

1 cup (240 g) tahini paste

½ to ¾ cup (120 to 180 ml) warm water

1 clove garlic, finely chopped or grated

¾ tsp kosher salt

1 Persian cucumber, finely diced

1 medium tomato, finely diced

½ preserved lemon, seeds removed, finely chopped, or the zest of ½ lemon

¼ cup (4 g) chopped fresh cilantro

¼ cup (25 g) chopped fresh mint leaves

2 tbsp (30 ml) olive oil, plus more for garnish

½ tsp sumac

¼ tsp Aleppo pepper

In a medium bowl, add the tahini paste, water, garlic and salt, and whisk until the sauce is a smooth, pourable consistency. The sauce will thicken at first but will smooth out as the whisking continues for another 1 to 3 minutes. Add more water as needed until the sauce becomes smooth and creamy. This can also be done in a small food processor or blender. Once smooth, pour the tahini sauce into a wide bowl.

In another bowl, toss the cucumber, tomato, preserved lemon, cilantro, mint and olive oil, and spoon the chopped salad in the center of the creamy tahini sauce. Garnish everything with a sprinkle of sumac, Aleppo pepper and a final drizzle of olive oil.

TIP: Just like natural nut butters, tahini can also have oil seperation. Before adding tahini to your recipes, give it a good stir so the oil is evenly mixed into the sesame seed paste.

CITRUS FENNEL SALAD WITH ORANGE BLOSSOM VINAIGRETTE

YIELDS
2
salads

Fennel and citrus are made for each other, and I suggest taking the time to shave the fennel as thin as you can. Thicker slices of fennel will have a stronger, more anise flavor, and the thinner the slices are, the milder they will be.

The unique flavor in the citrus vinaigrette comes from a touch of orange blossom water. Commonly, a splash would be found in sweet desserts such as baklava, but adding just a small amount to a vinaigrette enhances the other citrus notes in the salad. Orange blossom water can be overpowering and a little goes a very long way. Start small, and if you like the flavor, add a little more at a time.

CITRUS VINAIGRETTE

½ cup (120 ml) olive oil

2 tbsp (30 ml) grapefruit juice or lemon juice

2 tbsp (30 ml) honey

½ tsp orange blossom water

½ tsp kosher salt

SALAD

4 cups (80 g) arugula

1 small fennel bulb, shaved thin

1 grapefruit, peeled and cut into segments

2 tangerines or clementines, peeled and cut into segments

½ cup (87 g) pomegranate seeds

4 oz (113 g) crumbled goat cheese

For the vinaigrette, in the bottom of a wide salad bowl, add the olive oil, grapefruit juice, honey, orange blossom water and salt, and whisk to combine.

Add the arugula, fennel, grapefruit and tangerines, and toss the salad mixture with the dressing. Garnish the salad with pomegranate seeds and crumbled goat cheese right before serving.

TIP: If you're looking to make this salad ahead of time, whisk the vinaigrette and leave it at the bottom of a large salad bowl. Then pile in the ingredients, and when you're ready to serve, toss everything together.

SHREDDED KALE WITH ZA'ATAR RANCH AND CRISPY PROSCIUTTO

YIELDS
2 large salads

This salad is a play on a BLT, with a Mediterranean twist. Salty prosciutto crisps beautifully in the oven with the za'atar-seasoned chickpeas. For the kale, take the time to shred the leaves into thin ribbons, and massage the tangy yogurt dressing into the leaves very well, which will help tenderize the tougher greens.

KALE SALAD

1 (15.5-oz [439-g]) can chickpeas, drained, rinsed and dried well

1 tbsp (15 ml) olive oil

½ tsp kosher salt

1 tsp za'atar

4 to 6 slices prosciutto

1 bunch Lacinato kale, large stems removed and leaves shredded

1 pint (298 g) cherry tomatoes, halved

ZA'ATAR RANCH DRESSING

½ cup (120 ml) full-fat Greek yogurt

1 to 2 tbsp (15 to 30 ml) milk or nondairy milk substitute

2 tsp (7 g) za'atar

2 tsp (10 ml) lemon juice

1 tsp dried dill

1 tsp dried parsley

1 tsp dried chives

½ tsp onion powder

½ tsp garlic powder

½ tsp kosher salt

¼ tsp ground black pepper

Preheat the oven to 400°F (204°C). Scatter the chickpeas onto a baking sheet, drizzle with the olive oil and season with salt and za'atar. Give the chickpeas a good toss so all of the chickpeas are coated evenly with the spices. Lay the prosciutto slices around the chickpeas.

Roast the chickpeas and prosciutto for 20 to 22 minutes, until the prosciutto is crispy and the chickpeas are deep golden brown. Once done, remove and set aside while you make the rest of the salad.

For the za'atar ranch dressing, in a medium bowl, add the yogurt, milk, za'atar, lemon juice, dill, parsley, chives, onion powder, garlic powder, salt and pepper, and whisk to combine until smooth and creamy.

In a large bowl, add the shredded kale, and drizzle on a few tablespoons (45 ml) of za'atar ranch dressing. Using clean hands, massage the dressing into the kale leaves for a few minutes so the kale softens and all the leaves are evenly coated with the dressing.

To serve, scatter the cherry tomatoes, roasted chickpeas and crispy prosciutto onto the dressed kale with extra za'atar ranch dressing on the side.

 TIP: Look for Lacinato or dinosaur kale, which is more tender than curly kale.

SPICY CHOPPED TOMATO SALAD WITH POMEGRANATE

YIELDS
4
servings

Traditionally, you'll find chopped salads made simply with sweet tomatoes and fresh and crunchy cucumbers, which will always be a personal favorite. However, over the years, I've upgraded the classic chopped salad to add more contrast and layers of flavor and crunch.

When summer is at its peak, peaches and tomatoes are juicy and ripe and pair so well with the sweet and tangy notes of honey and pomegranate molasses. This is a great addition to add to Sheet Pan Salmon Shawarma (page 65) or to serve alongside other grilled meats and fish in the summertime.

If pomegranate molasses is not available, add 2 teaspoons (10 ml) balsamic vinegar, which will also offer a pop of tanginess.

2 peaches, pit removed and diced

2 medium vine tomatoes, seeds removed, diced

½ cup (87 g) pomegranate seeds

½ small Fresno chile, minced

2 tsp (10 ml) pomegranate molasses

2 tsp (10 ml) honey

1 tsp lemon juice

½ tsp kosher salt

2 to 4 sprigs fresh mint, leaves finely chopped

To a large bowl, add the peaches, tomatoes, pomegranate seeds and chile, and toss to combine.

Drizzle in the pomegranate molasses, honey and lemon juice, and season everything with salt. Taste for seasoning, and garnish with fresh mint.

 TIP: Look for in-season, sweet stone fruits such as peaches or nectarines. The sweeter the fruit is, the better the contrast will be with the spicy chile and tangy pomegranate molasses.

QUICK-PICKLED ONION SALAD WITH SUMAC

YIELDS
4
side salds

If you are looking for a condiment to punch up the flavors of proteins, this onion salad with sumac will be your favorite addition! Sumac is a tart and sour spice, coming from the sumac bush. You can find it dried near the spice section of most grocery stores, as it is becoming more popular in mainstream supermarkets.

Typically, this sumac onion salad is served alongside grilled meats, but I have added it to everything, including Mediterranean Watermelon Salad with Mint and Feta (page 159). This is a quick pickle and can be made up to 3 days ahead of time, though the red onions may change color from the acid, and that is totally okay.

½ medium red onion, thinly sliced

2 tbsp (30 ml) olive oil

1 tbsp (9 g) sumac

½ tsp kosher salt

Juice of 1 lemon

Small bunch fresh parsley, leaves finely chopped

To a bowl, add the onion, olive oil, sumac, salt, lemon juice and parsley, and mix to combine. Taste for seasoning and adjust as needed. Let the onion salad marinate for at least 10 minutes so all the flavors can meld together.

MARINATED ARTICHOKE SALAD WITH OREGANO AND BASIL

YIELDS
2
salads

Even if you don't have a lot of fresh produce around, you can still make a lively and flavorful salad. Canned artichokes and jarred bell peppers come in handy and transform otherwise simple ingredients into a delectable and filling side salad. Fresh basil and oregano help brighten the flavors, but in a pinch, dried basil and dried oregano work very well.

RED WINE VINAIGRETTE

½ cup (120 ml) olive oil

1 tbsp (15 ml) red wine vinegar

1 tbsp (15 ml) lemon juice

1 tsp honey

1 tsp Dijon mustard

½ tsp dried oregano

½ tsp kosher salt

ARTICHOKE SALAD

1 (14-oz [396-g]) can artichoke hearts, drained, large hearts cut in half or quarters

½ small red onion, thinly sliced

1 roasted bell pepper, thinly sliced

1 pint (298 g) cherry tomatoes, halved

2 to 3 sprigs fresh oregano, leaves removed

Small bunch fresh basil leaves, for garnish

Pinch of red pepper flakes, for garnish

In the bottom of a large bowl, add the olive oil, red wine vinegar, lemon juice, honey, Dijon, dried oregano and salt, and whisk to combine. Add the artichoke hearts, onion, bell pepper, cherry tomatoes and fresh oregano, and give everything a good mix, making sure all of the vegetables are coated with the vinaigrette.

Garnish the artichoke salad with fresh basil leaves and red pepper flakes.

GREEK-INSPIRED PANZANELLA WITH RED WINE VINAIGRETTE AND FETA

YIELDS
2
salads

There is nothing I love more than a crunchy, textured salad. Traditionally, panzanella is a rustic Italian salad made with leftover stale bread and various vegetables. In my version, I took a Greek-inspired approach with lots of briny flavors and ingredients. The vinaigrette is bright and zippy and doesn't skimp on the pepperoncini, which provides a nice vinegary bite.

This is a perfect salad to make ahead and to use up that stale bread. If you only have fresh bread, cut the bread into cubes and toast them in the oven for a few minutes until they're just dried out.

Serve alongside Greek Chicken with Rice and Olives (page 13).

½ loaf ciabatta or French bread, cut into 1-inch (2.5-cm) pieces

2 tbsp (30 ml) olive oil

1 head romaine, chopped

2 Persian cucumbers, cut into ½-inch (1.3-cm) cubes

1 cup (150 g) cherry tomatoes, halved

¼ cup (45 g) pitted Kalamata olives, roughly chopped

¼ cup (30 g) pepperoncini, roughly chopped

½ small red onion, thinly sliced

RED WINE VINAIGRETTE

½ cup (120 ml) olive oil

2 tbsp (30 ml) red wine vinegar

2 tsp (10 ml) honey

2 tsp (10 ml) Dijon mustard

¾ tsp dried oregano

½ tsp kosher salt

FOR SERVING

4 oz (113 g) crumbled feta cheese, for garnish

Fresh dill, for garnish

Preheat the oven to 400°F (204°C). In a large bowl, toss the cubed bread with the olive oil, and scatter it onto a baking sheet. Bake the bread cubes for about 10 minutes to dry out the bread. Once done, remove from the oven and set aside.

While the bread is toasting, make the red wine vinaigrette. In a small bowl or a Mason jar, add the olive oil, red wine vinegar, honey, Dijon, oregano and salt, and whisk or shake to combine.

In a wide bowl, arrange the romaine, Persian cucumbers, cherry tomatoes, Kalamata olives, pepperoncini, onion and bread cubes. Drizzle enough of the vinaigrette to lightly coat everything, and toss to combine. Add more dressing, if desired, but just enough to lightly coat all of the vegetables.

Right before serving, garnish the salad with crumbled feta cheese and fresh dill.

MEDITERRANEAN WATERMELON SALAD WITH MINT AND FETA

YIELDS
2 to 4
servings

You may not be able to resist the pungent flavors once you bite into this Mediterranean watermelon salad. Inspired by the Quick-Pickled Onion Salad with Sumac (page 152), the same flavors are added to sweet chunks of watermelon and salty and creamy feta. Sweet, fresh, juicy, tangy and salty, this refreshing salad has it all.

SALAD DRESSING

2 tbsp (30 ml) lime juice

1 tsp honey

½ tsp sumac, plus more for garnish

WATERMELON SALAD

½ red onion, very thinly sliced

4 cups (608 g) cubed watermelon

4 oz (113 g) cubed feta cheese

Fresh mint leaves, roughly chopped

In the bottom of a salad bowl, whisk the lime juice, honey and sumac together. Add the red onion and watermelon, and toss everything to combine, making sure the dressing evenly coats the watermelon and onion.

Before serving, add the cubed feta cheese and fresh mint, and give the salad one final toss, making sure to not disturb the feta too much. Garnish with additional sumac, if desired.

TURKISH SHEPHERD'S SALAD WITH FRESH HERBS AND SUMAC

YIELDS
2
salads

Turkish shepherd's salad, also called *coban salatasi*, is a rustic chopped salad utilizing sweet tomatoes, fresh cucumbers and a tangy dressing. The dressing is simple and bright and can be drizzled onto the vegetables as soon as you are done prepping. My slight twist includes adding a drizzle of aged balsamic, which gives the tangy and peppery flavors a hint of sweetness.

Thin-peeled Persian cucumbers are called for here, but you can use any other thin-skinned cucumber, such as English cucumbers. If only the more common, slicing cucumbers are available, peel the thicker skin and scoop out the watery seeds.

Serve alongside Lemony Za'atar Chicken and Potatoes (page 29) or Sheet Pan Salmon Shawarma (page 65).

2 medium vine tomatoes, cut into ½-inch (1.3-cm) chunks

1 Anaheim pepper, seeded, cut into ½-inch (1.3-cm) chunks

2 Persian cucumbers, cut into ½-inch (1.3-cm) chunks

½ red onion, thinly sliced

Small bunch fresh dill, roughly chopped

Small bunch fresh cilantro, roughly chopped

½ tsp dried mint

½ tsp sumac

2 tbsp (30 ml) olive oil

2 tbsp (30 ml) fresh lemon juice

2 tbsp (30 ml) aged balsamic vinegar

½ tsp kosher salt

Oil-cured olives, optional, for serving

To a large bowl, add the tomatoes, Anaheim pepper, cucumbers, onion, dill, cilantro, mint and sumac, and give the vegetables a gentle toss.

Pour in the olive oil, lemon juice, balsamic vinegar and salt, and give everything a good stir so all of the herbs and spices evenly coat the vegetables. Taste for seasoning, and adjust as needed. If desired, serve with oil-cured olives on the side for an extra salty bite.

CHUNKY BEET SALAD WITH WALNUTS AND CILANTRO VINAIGRETTE

YIELDS
2
servings

My love for beets runs deep, and I adore the sweet and earthy notes of ruby-red beets. If you love beets as much as I do, you will love this chunky salad. Inspired by a popular Turkish salad, the beets are simply dressed with tangy pomegranate molasses, bright cilantro vinaigrette and garnished with walnuts that add crunch and creaminess.

2 medium cooked beets, cut into cubes

2 tbsp (30 ml) pomegranate molasses

¼ cup (44 g) pomegranate seeds

½ tsp kosher salt

½ tsp Aleppo pepper

½ cup (59 g) chopped walnuts

CILANTRO VINAIGRETTE

¾ cup (12 g) fresh cilantro leaves, roughly chopped

1 small shallot, roughly chopped

1 clove garlic, roughly chopped

1 tbsp (15 ml) apple cider vinegar

¼ tsp kosher salt

½ cup (120 ml) olive oil

To a bowl, add the beets, pomegranate molasses, pomegranate seeds, salt, Aleppo pepper and walnuts, and toss to combine.

For the cilantro vinaigrette, in a small food processor or blender, add the cilantro, shallot, garlic, vinegar and salt, and pulse until finely chopped. While the food processor is running, stream in the olive oil until well incorporated and until all leaves have been finely chopped.

Arrange the beet salad on a platter, and drizzle with the cilantro vinaigrette.

TIP: Prepped and cooked beets are easily found in the produce section of most grocery stores. However, if you feel like roasting your own beets, wrap clean beets in foil, and bake at 400°F (204°C) for 45 minutes to an hour until easily pierced with a knife. Then peel and chop the beets as needed. Cooked beets can last up to 1 week in an airtight container in the refrigerator.

ACKNOWLEDGMENTS

Having the opportunity to write these acknowledgments a second time is truly another dream come true. You all make me a better person, and I am so lucky to have you in my life.

Firstly, my mom, whom I miss every single day and wish were here to see the new book. Thank you for always believing in me, cheering for me and telling every single person you met how proud you were of me. I think about you every single day and am so thankful you introduced me to the culture and experiences I get to write about. I miss you and love you.

To my best friend of more than twenty years, Dominee. You have helped me work on the first book and this one, and you are always here to get down to business. We have fun and eat well, and I am so lucky and blessed to have you in my life.

Lizzie, Jessica, Amanda, Josh and Maegan, thank you for being such wonderful friends. When we moved to Washington, we didn't know a single soul, and not only have you all taken us into your hearts and homes, but you have always been willing taste testers for any recipe I throw at you.

To my blog readers and The Little Ferraro Kitchen community, you make me excited to cook for you and with you. Thank you for being here, for cooking my recipes, for engaging conversation and for bringing my flavors into your homes. This is something I am forever grateful for. Thank you for being a part of this community.

To the team at Page Street, thank you for instilling trust in me, and for your honesty, patience and professionalism. It has been a pleasure to do this project with you all again.

And as with the first, I want to dedicate the last few words to my husband, my best friend and forever partner in life, Joe. You are my rock, and none of this would ever be possible without the love and respect I get from you every single day. We are a fantastic team, and I am so excited for what lies ahead. I love you so much.

ABOUT THE AUTHOR

Samantha Ferraro is the author of *The Weeknight Mediterranean Kitchen* and the blogger and creator of the food blog The Little Ferraro Kitchen, where she shares world cuisine recipes, spanning different cultures and ethnicities.

Her recipes have been shared with the *LA Times*, *The Huffington Post*, *Cosmopolitan* and *Women's Health*.

Samantha has lived in several major areas, including New York City, Hawaii, California and the Pacific Northwest, illustrating her diversity in culture and food. When Samantha isn't in the kitchen, she is out enjoying the beauty of the Pacific Northwest with her husband, Joe, in Bellingham, Washington.

INDEX